GARLAND STUDIES IN

ENTREPRENEURSHIP

edited by
STUART BRUCHEY
UNIVERSITY OF MAINE

A GARLAND SERIES

NEW VENTURE FORMATIONS IN UNITED STATES MANUFACTURING

THE ROLE OF INDUSTRY ENVIRONMENTS

THOMAS J. DEAN

GARLAND PUBLISHING, INC.
NEW YORK & LONDON / 1995

HD
9725
D36
1995

Library of Congress Cataloging-in-Publication Data

Dean, Thomas J., 1960–
    New venture formations in United States manufacturing : the
role of industry environments / Thomas J. Dean.
        p.   cm. — (Garland studies in entrepreneurship)
    Includes bibliographical references and index.
    ISBN 0-8153-2128-7 (alk. paper)
    1. United States—Manufacturing—Mathematical models.
2. New business enterprises—United States—Mathematical
models. 3. Industrial location—United States—Mathematical
models. 4. Entrepreneurship—United States—Mathematical
models. I. Title. II. Series.
HD9725.D36 1995
338.7'67'0973—dc20
                                                                95-38868

To My Father

CONTENTS

LIST OF TABLES . . . . *ix*
LIST OF FIGURES . . . . *xi*

CHAPTER I: INTRODUCTION *3*
    Scope of the Book *7*
    Academic Contributions *9*
    Concepts and Definitions *10*

CHAPTER II: REVIEW OF THE LITERATURE *15*
    Industry Disequilibrium, Market Opportunity
        and Entrepreneurship *15*
    Industry Dynamics *38*
    Organizational Inertia *44*
    Ecological Models of Organizational Foundings *48*
    Entry Barriers *52*
    Chapter Summary *70*

CHAPTER III: THEORETICAL DEVELOPMENT *71*
    Theoretical Development and Propositions *73*
    Development of Testable Hypotheses *89*
    Theoretical Summary *101*

CHAPTER IV: RESEARCH DESIGN AND
    METHODOLOGY *103*
    Regression Model, Hypotheses, and Research Method *103*
    Sample Description *108*
    Data Sources *110*
    Variable Measures *114*
    Chapter Summary *123*

CHAPTER V: RESULTS *125*
    Descriptive Statistics *125*

Bivariate Relationships *132*
Regression Results *146*
Validity of Regression Assumptions *151*
Chapter Summary *159*

CHAPTER VI: DISCUSSION OF RESULTS,
LIMITATIONS, AND FUTURE RESEARCH *161*
Discussion of Results *161*
Limitations *172*
Implications for Future Research *174*

BIBLIOGRAPHY *177*
INDEX *195*

LIST OF TABLES

Table II-1:   Summary of Theoretical Arguments
              on Entrepreneurship *35*

Table II-2:   Empirical Studies of the Relation Between
              Advertising and Entry *58*

Table II-3:   Empirical Studies of the Relation Between
              Capital Requirements and Entry *63*

Table II-4:   Empirical Studies of the Relation Between
              Industry Concentration and Entry *65*

Table II-5:   Empirical Studies of the Relation Between
              Industry Growth and Entry *66*

Table II-6:   Empirical Studies of the Relation Between
              Industry Profitability and Entry *67*

Table II-7:   Empirical Studies of the Relation Between
              Technological Intensity and Entry *69*

Table IV-1:   Hypotheses *106*
Table IV-2:   Comparisons *109*

Table V-1:   Descriptive Statistics *126*
Table V-2:   Highest and Lowest Levels of New Venture
              Formation *128*
Table V-3:   Correlation Matrix *145*
Table V-4:   Regression Results *147*

Table VI-1:   Summary of Results *164*

LIST OF FIGURES

Figure II-1:   Kirzner's Model of Entreneurship 24
Figure II-2:   Rizzo's Conceptualization of Disequilibrium
                and Entrepreneurship 25
Figure II-3:   Leibenstein's X-Inefficiency and Entrepreneurship . 27
Figure II-4:   Knight's Conception of Entrepreneurship 28
Figure II-5:   Schumpeter's Creative Destruction 29
Figure II-6:   Rosen's Conceptualization of Entrepreneurship . . . 30
Figure II-7:   Penrose, and Large and Small Firm Entreneurship . 32
Figure II-8:   Sandberg and Yip's Models of Disequilibrium
                and Entrepreneurship 34

Figure III-1:   An Integrative Conceptual Model
                of New Venture Formation 72
Figure III-2:   Illustration of Propositions 1, 2, and 3 78
Figure III-3:   Illustration of Propositions 3 and 4 80
Figure III-4:   Alternative Exploitations of Market
                Opportunities 81
Figure III-5:   Simplistic Predictions of the Exploitation
                of Market Opportunity 82
Figure III-6:   Conceptualization of Austrian and
                Schumpeterian Entrepreneurs 88
Figure III-7:   Empirical Model of New Venture Formation 102

Figure V-1:   Descriptive Statistics and Histogram for NVF . . . 127
Figure V-2:   Descriptive Statistics and Histogram for LOGNVF 130
Figure V-3:   PCTGRTH Scatterplots 133
Figure V-4:   NICHEDYN Scatterplots 134
Figure V-5:   VOL Scatterplots 135
Figure V-6:   RD Scatterplots 136
Figure V-7:   ADV Scatterplots 137
Figure V-8:   EXCAP Scatterplots 138
Figure V-9:   LOGCR Scatterplots 139
Figure V-10:   C4 Scatterplots 140
Figure V-11:   WTDAGE Scatterplots 141
Figure V-12:   SZ Scatterplots 142
Figure V-13:   Union Scatterplots 143

Figure V-14: Standardized Predicted Values Vs. Standardized
          Results *152*
Figure V-15: Histogram of Standardized Regression Residual .. *154*
Figure V-16: Normal Probability Plot Based on Standardized
          Residuals *155*

New Venture Formations in
United States Manufacturing

I

INTRODUCTION

ENTREPRENEURSHIP AND ENTREPRENEURSHIP RESEARCH

The entrepreneur, long absent from the analyses of mainstream economists, has made undeniable contributions to economic development in the 1980's. In fact, the eighties became the decade of the entrepreneur (Drucker, 1985), and the attention directed toward entrepreneurship rose to peak heights as policy-makers looked to entrepreneurism to stimulate economic growth. Books were published, magazines initiated, and even academic courses were offered on the pragmatics of entrepreneurship. As we entered the nineties, entrepreneurship remained at the forefront of popularity and was looked to as a way to emerge from economic stagnation into prosperity.

The extensive and broadly based interest in entrepreneurship has been justified by empirical evidence regarding the role of entrepreneurship in economic and social development. Empirical studies have shown a link between entrepreneurship and job formation, technological innovation, economic efficiency, export rates, competitive vibrancy, and other economic variables (Timmons, 1982). Drucker (1985) argues that it has been entrepreneurship that has overpowered the Kondratief cycle for the United States.

In the academic community, the subject of entrepreneurship has been investigated by academics from a broad array of research perspectives and disciplines (Hisrich, 1988; Low & MacMillan, 1988). Psychologists, for example, have studied the individual characteristics associated with entrepreneurs (McClelland, 1961; Brockhaus, 1982). Similarly, sociologists have examined the socio-cultural influences on an individual's propensity and ability to become an entrepreneur

3

(Stinchcombe, 1965; Weber, 1930). Population ecologists have viewed
the entrepreneur as the creator of variation in organizational forms
(Delacroix & Carroll, 1983; Aldrich & Wiedenmayer, 1991; Hannan &
Freeman, 1977). Finally, economists have pondered the role of the
entrepreneur in economic development and in the determinants of the
rates of business creation (Schumpeter, 1934; Kirzner, 1973; Baumol,
1986).

Yet despite the popularity of entrepreneurship and its
acceptance as an important factor in economic development (Baumol,
1986), an understanding of the nature of entrepreneurship has remained
elusive. Economists, by and large, have experienced difficulty in
identifying, describing, and understanding the determinants of
entrepreneurship (Baumol, 1968). Management researchers have argued
that the field continues to remain in its infancy despite an increase in
the quantity and quality of research performed (Sexton, 1988; Sexton,
1987). Researchers cannot even arrive at a consistent definition of the
entrepreneur (Gartner, 1988; Kilby, 1971; VanderWerf and Brush,
1989), and recent criticisms of the "trait" approach to entrepreneurship
have questioned the value of researchers' traditional concentration on
the characteristics of entrepreneurs (Aldrich & Wiedenmayer, 1991;
Aldrich, 1990).

This unfortunate state of affairs in entrepreneurial research has
not been due to the lack of accomplishment on the part of researchers,
but has resulted from a number of other factors. First, it is widely
acknowledged that entrepreneurship is a multifaceted, complex, and
elusive subject (Gartner, 1989; Kilby, 1971). Second, the field lacks a
well-developed theoretical base and/or paradigm which researchers can
use to focus their inquiries (Carsrud, Olm, & Eddy, 1986; Wortman,
1987; Cheah, 1990). Hisrich recognizes the problematic nature of the
lack of a theoretical base: "Only when a solid theoretical foundation is
established will entrepreneurship gain respectability as an established
academic discipline" (1988: 4). Moreover, the broad scope of the
phenomenon and the lack of theory has constrained researchers from
arriving at a consistent definition (Brockhaus & Horwitz, 1986; Sexton
& Smilor, 1986, Wortman, 1987; Gartner, 1988, 1990). This lack of a
singular definition has created difficulties in sample selection (Gartner,
1989); has resulted in the use of samples which are are not comparable
across studies (VanderWerf & Brush, 1989; Cooper & Dunkelberg,
1987); and has impeded the progress of the field (Low & MacMillan,
1988; Cheah, 1990). Finally, the dearth of data at the firm and industry
level has inhibited researchers' ability to study entrepreneurship.

Historically, research on entrepreneurship has overwhelmingly focused upon the characteristics of entrepreneurs (Hornady & Churchill, 1987; Wortman, 1987). This "traits approach" proposes a relationship between entrepreneurial activity and the characteristics of entrepreneurs (Aldrich & Wiedenmayer, 1991; Aldrich, 1990). That is, the phenomenon of entrepreneurship is said to be a function of the psychological and demographic characteristics of individuals within society. Research on entrepreneurial characteristics has generally taken one of two approaches (Gartner, 1989). The first approach is to compare entrepreneurs to non-entrepreneurs relative to a variety of psychological and demographic variables, and then to conclude that certain of these traits are associated with entrepreneurial propensity. In short, entrepreneurship is a function of the entrepreneur. The second approach is to compare different classifications of entrepreneurs to each other. For example, researchers compare the traits of successful entrepreneurs to those of unsuccessful entrepreneurs in order to distinguish between effective entrepreneurial characteristics and ineffective ones (Gartner, 1989).

Despite the significant accomplishments of trait-oriented research, some authors have argued that this stream of research has hit a dead end in its potential for further contributions to the understanding of entrepreneurship (Aldrich, 1990). In addition, the concentration on entrepreneurial characteristics has resulted in the neglect of other important topics (Aldrich & Wiedenmayer, 1991; Wortman, 1987). More specifically, the emphasis on entrepreneurial characteristics has kept attention away from the complete investigation of the extent and causes of new venture creation. This "rates" approach (Aldrich & Wiedenmayer, 1991;) emphasizes the social, economic, and political environmental conditions which influence the rates of foundings (Aldrich, 1990; Aldrich & Wiedenmayer, 1991). Wortman (1987) observes that little research (empirical and theoretical) has been performed on the environments for entrepreneurship.

> Some authors have argued that investigation of the causes of variations in the rates of venture formations is a more fruitful area for investigation than the study of entrepreneurial characteristics (Aldrich & Wiedenmayer, 1991).

In short, the central purpose of the rates approach is to investigate the extent and causes of variance in rates of foundings (Aldrich & Wiedenmayer, 1991). Consequently, this perspective focuses on the determinants of business formations. Studies on the determinants of formation rates can be classified according to the source of variance which they attempt to explain.

Some studies of business foundings attempt to explain variance in founding rates across geographical regions or societies. Studies analyzing variance across regions or societies usually examine supply determinants of business formations. Supply factors (sometimes termed "push" factors (Shapero & Sokol, 1982)) refer to the "non-materialistic, inner, psychic" motivations of individuals as well as the "larger systems of sanctions based on the society's value and status hierarchy, which in its entirety will determine the extent of entrepreneurial activity" (Kilby, 1971: 4). Some authors have expanded this definition to include social structural variables that impact the ability of individuals to initiate ventures (Stinchcombe, 1965; Pennings, 1982). Typical supply variables include the protestant ethic (Weber, 1930); need for achievement (McClelland, 1961); creativity (Hagen, 1962), alertness (Kirzner, 1973; Gilad, 1982); cultural values and social sanctions (Cochran, 1971); and social structural variables such as literacy, education, urbanization, and a money economy (Stinchcombe, 1965). (See Bruno & Tybejee, 1985; Kilby, 1971; Pennings, 1980 for further discussions of supply determinants.) Empirical studies of supply variables include those of Pennings (1982), who attempts to explain the variance of foundings across urban areas; Baumol (1986), who examines the sources of variance in entrepreneurship across nations; and McClelland (1961), who studies variation in foundings across societies, using a traits approach.

Other studies have attempted to explain the variance in rates of business formations across industries or populations of organizations. Studies analyzing variance across industries or populations usually focus on demand determinants of venture creation. Demand determinants concern the monetary incentives which exist within the economic system (Glade, 1967; Kilby, 1971), and have been referred to as "conditions defining the potential opportunity structure" (Glade, 1967: 250). Individuals wishing to optimize economic rewards will pursue such opportunities through the formation of a business venture. Demand factors might also be termed "pull" factors (Glade, 1967; Shapero & Sokol, 1982) since they attract individuals to initiate new businesses.

Overall, emphasis on entrepreneurial characteristics by entrepreneurship researchers has resulted in the empirical and theoretical neglect of the study of rates of business formations, and, in particular, of demand determinants of business formations (Aldrich & Wiedenmayer, 1991). Few empirical studies have been performed on the demand aspects of entrepreneurial activity. Yet, researchers see demand determinants as being at least as important as supply determinants (Glade, 1967). An adequate supply of entrepreneurs would yield little without opportunities upon which they can act.

Exceptions to the lack of empirical research on demand determinants include the research of population ecologists (i.e., Delacroix & Carroll, 1983; Hannan & Freeman, 1987; Tucker, Singh, & Meinhard, 1990), and studies by economists analyzing entry barriers (i.e., Bain, 1956; Acs & Audretsch, 1989; Harrigan, 1981). Some unique studies which might be classified as demand determinant studies include those of Creedy and Johnson (1983), who find a relation between formation rates and the comparative expected income from self-employment; and Highfield and Smiley (1987) who examine the macro-economic determinants of entry. Still, the implications of such empirical studies on demand determinants have largely been ignored by entrepreneurship researchers.

SCOPE OF THE BOOK

In order to help overcome the paucity of research on demand determinants of business formations, this manuscript investigates the variation in rates of new venture initiations across manufacturing industries. Since demand determinants of new business formations concern the monetary incentives of entrepreneurship, investigations of pull factors are perhaps best approached from an economic perspective. However, mainstream economists have experienced difficulty in describing and explaining entrepreneurship. Part of the difficulty has resulted from economists' somewhat narrow focus on formal analytical models of general equilibrium. Within the theory of general equilibrium, the entrepreneur serves no purpose other than that of the rationally optimizing manager (Rizzo, 1979; Hayek, 1948; Kirzner, 1973). Entrepreneurship, by its idiosyncratic nature, is not easily subjected to the deterministic analysis usually applied to general equilibrium (Baumol, 1968; Kirzner, 1973).

Yet some economists have analyzed the entrepreneur with a great deal of effectiveness. Theories of the Austrian school (i.e., Kirzner, 1973; Mises, 1949; Hayek, 1948), and those of Schumpeter (1934), Leibenstein (1979), and Knight (1921), for example, have been invaluable to the current understanding of entrepreneurship. By modifying many of the assumptions of general equilibrium theory, many of these authors have been successful in describing the phenomenon of entrepreneurship. Austrian economists have been especially effective in presenting a theoretical foundation upon which a model of demand determinants of entrepreneurship might be based. Sandberg (1986: 5) argues that "the Austrian School has provided the key insights into the role and reasoning of the entrepreneur." In short, Austrian economic theory emphasizes the role of market disequilibrium in creating economic opportunities and thereby encouraging entrepreneurship.

Based on Austrian and other perspectives on market disequilibrium, this book proposes a model of new venture formation in dynamic markets. It focuses on the environmental factors which impact rates of entrepreneurship in industries and argues that more dynamic industries will contain more profit opportunities and therefore exhibit a greater degree of entrepreneurship and new venture creation. However, the prediction of rates of new venture formations requires consideration of two additional constructs: entry barriers and organizational inertia. In the industrial organization economics literature, entry barriers have been hypothesized to have a negative impact on the entry of firms into an industry (Bain, 1956). In addition, organization theorists, population ecologists, and others have suggested that inertial characteristics of existing firms can prohibit their movement towards entrepreneurial opportunities, thus leaving opportunities open for exploitation by new firms. In short, industrial organization economics and organization theory bring valuable insights into the determinants of new venture formations across industries. Dynamic industry environments create opportunities for alert entrepreneurs, while entry barriers act to constrain the creation of new firms. Inertial properties of existing firms constrain them from exploiting available opportunities and thereby encourage the formation of new firms.

In order to facilitate examination of the research, the book is organized into six chapters. This introductory chapter discusses the state of entrepreneurship research, provides a brief overview of the scope of the book, and presents a number of important concepts and definitions.

The second chapter provides a literature review of theoretical and empirical research that is relevant to understanding the demand determinants of entrepreneurship. The chapter begins with a review of theoretical research on market disequilibrium and the nature of entrepreneurship. Then, economic and organization theory concepts of industry dynamics are investigated. Perspectives on the nature of organizational inertia and its effect on new venture formations are then discussed. Finally, industrial economics theories of entry barriers are explored.

The third chapter utilizes the ideas discussed in the literature review to build a theoretical model of new venture formations in manufacturing industries. The chapter is divided into two major sections. The first section develops a number of general propositions on the relationships between new venture formation and industry dynamics, entry barriers, and organizational inertia. The second section is devoted to translating a number of the propositions into specific, testable hypotheses.

Chapter IV presents the research design and methodology used to test the theoretical model developed in Chapter III. The chapter describes the regression model and methodology, and addresses the nature of the sample, data sources, and measures.

Chapter V presents the results of the data analysis without interpretation or extensive discussion. The chapter begins with a descriptive examination of each of the variables and then moves into presentation of the regression results. It concludes with an analysis of the validity of the regression assumptions.

The final chapter summarizes the results of the study and interprets the findings relative to prior entrepreneurship research. The limitations of the study are discussed, and a number of recommendations for future research are suggested.

In summary, this research examines the demand determinants of new venture formations in manufacturing industries. It integrates Austrian economics, industrial organization economics, and organization theory to arrive at a model of new venture formation which is based on industry dynamics, entry barriers, and organizational inertia.

ACADEMIC CONTRIBUTIONS

Theoretically, this study makes a number of important contributions. First, it is well grounded in a theoretical foundation which represents a unique integration of a number of perspectives on entrepreneurship, new venture formation, and entry. Specifically, the theoretical model utilizes ideas from Austrian economics, industrial organization economics, and organization theory. Following Austrian and other perspectives on disequilibrium, the model emphasizes the role of market dynamics in creating opportunities which encourage entrepreneurship and new venture formation. Despite important arguments which imply such relationships exist, prior theoretical and empirical research has failed to examine the specific implications of these ideas. The present study explicitly addresses the role of market dynamics in increasing new venture formations and provides an empirical test of this relationship. Moreover, important and empirically validated research on entry barriers is applied to the understanding of new venture formations. While the concept of entry is distinct from the phenomenon of new venture formation, entry theory has important implications for explaining the determinants of new venture formations. Despite significant findings on the relationship between entry barriers and rates of industry entry, the ideas of industrial organization economists have not been extensively utilized in prior entrepreneurship research.

The present study also applies the concept of organizational inertia to the understanding of new venture formations. Prior research has implied that a relation between inertia and entrepreneurship does exist, but there is a general lack of both theoretical and empirical research that addresses this connection.

Empirically, this study is unique in several respects. First, the research uses an underutilized collection of data on rates of new business formations at the industry level. Moreover, the study combines this data with a number of additional secondary data sources to create an extensive and unique database of industry-level variables.

CONCEPTS AND DEFINITIONS

Entrepreneurship

Researchers have been notoriously inconsistent in their definitions of entrepreneurship (Brockhaus & Horwitz, 1986; Sexton & Smilor, 1986, Wortman, 1987; Gartner, 1988). Definitions have emphasized a broad range of activities including creating organizations (Gartner, 1988); carrying out new combinations (Schumpeter, 1934); exploiting opportunities (Kirzner, 1973); bearing uncertainty (Knight, 1921); bringing together factors of production (Say, 1803); and others (See Long, 1983). The present theory will emphasize the function of entrepreneurs in exploiting opportunities within the existing economic system through the initiation of productive activities. Therefore, the following definition focuses on the productive and opportunity-seizing activities of entrepreneurs.

> Entrepreneurship is the combination of productive inputs with the purpose of taking advantage of market opportunities within the extant economic system.

This definition is similar to that proposed by Aldrich & Wiedenmayer (1991), who argue that entrepreneurship involves the mobilization of resources in pursuit of opportunities. The function of the entrepreneur as exploiter of opportunities is also recognized by Kirzner (1973), Mises (1949), Penrose (1963), and others. Timmons (1990) also considers entrepreneurship to be the process of creating or seizing an opportunity. This definition does not preclude already existing organizations from the function of entrepreneurship. Therefore, it is appropriate to include corporate entrepreneurship within the realm of the present definition.

New Venture Formations

Despite the broad definition of entrepreneurship provided above, the present study focuses on new venture formations which can be considered to be a segment of the phenomenon of entrepreneurship.

> New venture formation represents the combination of productive inputs by new, independent (of any existing organization), profit-oriented organizations with the purpose of taking advantage of market opportunities within the extant economic system.

This definition excludes diversification efforts of existing organizations as well as the creation of non-profit-oriented organizations. As such, Gartner's (1988) terminology, the creation of new organizations is perhaps too broad to be used for the purposes of the present research. Synonymous terms for new venture formation that will be used throughout this book include new-firm formation, new venture creation, new firm entrepreneurship, and other similar terms.

Entry

Readers of this book should be careful to distinguish between the concepts of entry and new venture formations. Although relevant to the study of new venture formations, entry is not the ultimate concern of the present study. Entry can be seen as a broader concept than new venture formations within an industry, and is inclusive of existing firms diversifying into an industry and new firms created to serve the relevant industry. In short, entry is a broader concept than new venture formations and concerns the act of a firm serving an industry which it did not serve before.

Economic Profits and Entrepreneurial Rents

Rumelt (1987) introduces the concept of entrepreneurial rents to reflect the monetary reward which an entrepreneur creates by initiating a venture in an uncertain environment.

> Entrepreneurial rent represents "the difference between a venture's ex-post value (or payment stream) and the ex-ante cost (or value) of the resources combined to form the venture" (Rumelt, 1987: 143).

Entrepreneurial rent therefore accrues due to the uncertainty the entrepreneur bears in combining resources prior to knowing the ex-post value of the combined resources. While Rumelt's concept of entrepreneurial rent fits well with the theoretical arguments presented herein, it is more parsimonious to use the term "economic profits" to reflect the return that the entrepreneur creates.

> Economic profits represent the return above and beyond all costs incurred in producing a product including the cost of capital (normal return to capital) and other implicit costs (Maurice & Smithson, 1985: 296).

In order to maintain parallel semantics with other studies on disequilibrium and entrepreneurship, the term "economic profits" rather than "entrepreneurial rents" will be used. Any reference to profits should be interpreted as meaning *economic* profits.

Industry or Market

The definition and specification of what is meant by a market is crucial to economic and organizational research. Yet, the exact definition of markets and industries has been a source of continual debate (Nightingale, 1978). For present purposes, the definition of market agrees with that of Scherer (1980). Scherer views markets as being defined according to the substitution possibilities on both the demand and supply side. On the demand side, industry membership is determined by whether the products that firms produce "are good substitutes for one another in the eyes of buyers" (Scherer, 1980: 60). On the supply side, firms can be seen as being of the same industry if they "employ essentially similar skills and equipment and if they can quickly move into each others' product lines should the profit lure beckon" (Scherer, 1980: 60). Scherer's view of markets is appropriate to the present study because it recognizes both demand and supply side issues of markets. This is contrary to some definitions of markets which focus only on buyers and their nature (Nightingale, 1978). For empirical purposes, a market will be formally designated according to the U.S. Department of Commerce Standard Industrial Classification (S.I.C.) system. A market is defined as a four-digit S.I.C. classification. While this system is far from perfect (Scherer, 1980), it does represent the basis for the collection of data which is utilized in this study. An industry will be considered synonymous with a market.

Sub-industry-level groupings of consumers with similar enough characteristics to enable aggregation, yet having demand characteristics dissimilar to other groups of customers within the industry, shall be termed *niches*, or *sub-industry-level demand*. Industries can be viewed as serving an aggregation of niches. For empirical purposes, five-digit S.I.C. classifications will represent niches.

Market Change

Market change refers to the alteration of the market on either the demand or supply side. Put in terms of popular demand and supply curve comparative statics analysis, industry change can be seen as any factor which might result in a shift in either the demand or the supply curve. Among the exogenous variables which economists have identified to impact the demand curve are the incomes of consumers, prices of related commodities, consumer tastes and preferences, and expectations about future prices (Maurice & Smithson, 1985). The level of technology, prices of inputs, and future expectations about the price of the commodity are usually associated with shifts in the supply curve (Maurice & Smithson, 1985). Five general categories of market change include: 1) increases in demand, 2) modification of demand, 3) technology development, 4) new sources of supply, and 5) political/regulatory change. Industry change, market dynamics, disequilibrating forces and other similar terms are synonymous with market change.

Market Opportunity

Market opportunities are productive possibilities which, when acted upon, can yield profits for economic actors. Market opportunities are characterized by incentives which exist within the market. Producers, for example, could produce a given product at a lower cost, sell at the present market price, and earn economic profits. The existence of market opportunities implies a state of market disequilibrium.

Entry Barriers

Entry barriers are factors which give incumbent firms an asymmetrical advantage in serving a market and therefore act to exclude entrants (Gilbert, 1989). More formally, "a barrier to entry may be defined as a cost of producing (at some or every level of output) which must be borne by a firm which seeks to enter an industry but is not borne by firms already in the industry" (Stigler, 1968: 67).

Organizational Inertia

Stinchcombe (1965) suggests that organizational forms tend to become institutionalized and that the basic structural characteristics of organizations are stable over time. Hannan and Freeman propose that this "structural inertia" reflects an organization's inability to adapt (1977), and that organizations rarely make radical changes in strategy and structure in reaction to environmental threats (1984). Both internal and external inertial pressures are said to impact an organization's ability to adapt (Hannan & Freeman, 1984). Romanelli and Tushman (1986) view inertia as the extent to which organizations persist in their basic patterns of activity regardless of changes in their environment. Miller and Friesen (1980) perceive inertia as organizational momentum whereby linkages perpetuate the status quo and make reversal in direction rare. The present definition of inertia builds on these ideas but adds the idea that inertia is recognized when firms do not move to opportunities within a market. Authors who address the ideas of inertia (though they do not necessarily refer to it as inertia) relative to market opportunities include Kirzner (1979), Leibenstein (1979), and Penrose (1963). In short, organizational inertia is the failure of organizations to move toward market opportunities which exist at disequilibrium.

II

REVIEW OF THE LITERATURE

Chapter Overview

A number of theoretical perspectives have been used to explain the determinants of new venture formations. Sociologists and psychologists have done an excellent job in delineating the supply determinants of business formations. However, economists, organizational theorists, and population ecologists provide the best understanding of demand determinants. Within these disciplines, three theoretical approaches have been especially helpful in explaining demand determinants of new venture formation. Austrian economists and others have emphasized the function of market dynamics and disequilibrium in encouraging entrepreneurship. Industrial organization economists have provided a strong theoretical basis regarding the factors which inhibit the entry of both existing and new firms in industries. Finally, organization theorists and population ecologists have suggested that the inertial properties of existing organizations may encourage entrepreneurial activity and the formation of ventures. In the discussion below, the advances relative to each of these conceptual approaches are discussed. First, the literature on the relationship between market dynamics, market disequilibrium, and entrepreneurship will be explored. Then, the ideas of organization theorists on market dynamics and organizational inertia are presented. Finally, a review of entry barrier theory is provided.

INDUSTRY DISEQUILIBRIUM, MARKET OPPORTUNITY, AND ENTREPRENEURSHIP

Numerous authors have suggested a relationship between the dynamics of industries, a state of disequilibrium, and entrepreneurship (i.e., Mises,

1949; Kirzner, 1973; Leibenstein, 1979; Knight, 1921; Yip, 1982). Yet, most of these authors concentrate on the broader concept of entrepreneurship and do not exclusively address new venture formation. As such, they have hypothesized a causal linkage between the rate of change occurring in an industry and the extent of entrepreneurship, where entrepreneurship is generally defined as the movement towards market opportunity by any economic actor (existing or new firms). Other things equal, their arguments might be extended to suggest a positive relationship between market change, disequilibrium, and the creation of new ventures. In the review below, however, the theoretical contributions of these authors will be reviewed relative to the broader concept of entrepreneurship.

Many of the arguments presented below represent seminal works on the subject of entrepreneurship. It is interesting to note that, despite the diverse sources, the common theme of industry dynamics and disequilibrium runs through most of the literature cited. The central point of these writings is that market change creates market opportunity and thereby stimulates entrepreneurship. While many of the conceptual arguments emanate from economic perspectives, most do not fit within popular neo-classical equilibrium analysis. Instead, these authors have found it necessary to remove many of the traditional assumptions of equilibrium theory to arrive at a conceptualization of entrepreneurship.

The section which follows begins with a discussion of why general equilibrium theory has not been useful in explaining the phenomenon of entrepreneurship and discusses the assumptions which must be mitigated before a conceptualization of entrepreneurship can emerge. Next, the thoughts of Austrian economists, Leibenstein, Knight, Penrose, Schumpeter, Rosen, and others are presented and explored. The perspectives of these authors are then summarized relative to ideas on industry dynamism, organizational inertia, entrepreneurship, and new venture formation.

General Equilibrium Theory

The assumption set of efficient market theory. While economists recognize the importance of the entrepreneur to economic growth, thorough analysis of the entrepreneurial role in economic theory has been "scanty" and almost "totally absent" (Baumol, 1968: 66). Mainstream economists, by and large, have experienced difficulty in identifying, describing, and understanding the determinants of entrepreneurship and have occasionally admitted their inadequacy in dealing with the entrepreneur's role in the economy (Baumol, 1968).

As Baumol (1983: 29) states, "The subject of entrepreneurship looms as a continuing reproach to the theory of the firm and to the formal analysis of economic growth."

It is curious that the entrepreneur has been so neglected in the writings of mainstream economists. A number of factors may account for the absence. To some extent, the study of the entrepreneur may be outside the domain of the economist (Greenfield & Strickon, 1981). The key to entrepreneurship rests, in part, in the individual characteristics and cultural influences which lead to the entrepreneurial decision.

Limitations on economic explanations of entrepreneurship have also arisen from a somewhat narrow focus on formal analytical models of general economic equilibrium. Within the theory of general equilibrium, the entrepreneur has little, if any, role to play. Apparently, the entrepreneur serves no purpose other than that of the rationally optimizing manager (Rizzo, 1979; Hayek, 1948; Kirzner, 1973). Yet, the entrepreneur has been viewed as performing more than the managerial role of overseeing the efficiency of a continuing operation (Baumol, 1968). Entrepreneurship, by its very nature, is not easily subjected to the deterministic analysis usually applied to general equilibrium (Baumol, 1968; Kirzner, 1973). Consequently, mainstream economics has tended away from consideration of the entrepreneur.

Yet some less mainstream economists have treated the entrepreneur with a great deal of effectiveness. Theories of the Austrian School (i.e., Kirzner, 1973; Mises, 1949; Hayek, 1948), and those of Schumpeter (1934), Leibenstein (1979), and Knight (1921), for example, have been invaluable to the current understanding of entrepreneurship. Such economic theories (which have been successful at explaining the phenomenon of entrepreneurship) have found it necessary to remove many of the conditions of general equilibrium theory. Three classical economic assumptions must be modified in order to arrive at a viable theory of the entrepreneur. The following paragraphs turn to an examination of these three assumptions.

The economic model of general equilibrium has a number of definitive conditions (assumptions). The first condition is that the *products within a market are homogeneous* (Hayek, 1948). In other words, little, if any, differences exist between the characteristics of the products sold by each market participant. As such, buyers distinguish between alternative offerings solely on the basis of price. Second, the neoclassical model emphasizes the *static quality of markets* whereby any changes in supply or demand characteristics are quickly and efficiently matched by equilibrating reactions of consumers and/or producers.

Rapid equilibration depends, in part, on an additional condition of perfectly competitive markets, having *complete information* (Hayek, 1948). Consumers have perfect knowledge of market offerings, and producers have complete information on market characteristics and production technologies. The outcome of these three conditions is that price instantaneously moves to marginal cost and no economic profit is attainable. (In the remainder of this study, profits refer to income above and beyond the cost of production, including interest and a normal return to capital). In addition, the quantity supplied is equal to the quantity demanded, and the market clears. The entrepreneur is no more than an allocator of productive resources with no opportunity for economic profit generation.

   While it is easy to see that the contemporary model of perfect competition is likely to be inaccurate due to the unrealistic nature of its assumptions, modification of these assumptions makes deterministic predictions difficult. Nonetheless, some authors have attempted to understand the implications of removing or modifying the various assumptions of the model (see, for example, Kirzner, 1973; Leibenstein, 1979; Knight, 1921). Such theories are based upon a view of markets which do not fit the neoclassical ideal and have moved from consideration of static, homogeneous markets with complete information to dynamic heterogeneous markets which are characterized by incomplete information. The implications of modifying these three traditional market assumptions are presented below, starting with heterogeneous demand.

   Heterogeneous demand and supply. The removal of the assumption of homogeneous supply and demand has a number of implications for the character of markets. Within economics, the basic unit of analysis is the industry. Yet variations in product offerings within an industry can be quite extensive (McGee, 1985). Differences in quality, features, and associated service levels are pervasive. In most markets, consumers are not identical in the characteristics they desire in products. As such, it is problematic to draw a single demand curve to characterize a group of consumers who vary significantly in their judgements of the best attributes of a product or group of products. Rather, it may be more appropriate to conceive of multiple demand curves within a single industry. While multiple demand curves remain distinct from one another, it is inherent to their nature that some cross-price elasticity will exist. The relation of separate demand curves within a single industry implies that products within an industry are substitutable for one another, yet separate enough to warrant individual demand curves rather than a singular all-encompassing one that ignores differences between individual demand curves.

Such sub-industry-level demand curves have often been termed "niches" by strategic management researchers (Zammuto, 1988; Bedeian & Zammuto, 1991). Bedeian and Zammuto (1991) define an industry niche as a resource space within which organizations can operate and survive. While this conception of niches is parallel to the present definition of multiple demand curves, it is broader since it considers the resources available to producers within the niche. A niche is "bounded by resource opportunities and constraints" such as "consumer demand, technological development, government policy and so on" (Bedeian & Zammuto 1991: 361).

The presence of differences in demand curves within an industry (heterogeneous demand) implies that some producers will attempt to serve that heterogeneity through product differentiation. Thus, the existence of heterogeneous demand will lead to heterogeneous supply whereby producers offer products which vary from those of other producers according to the desires of separate demand groups. This is the central argument of Porter (1980, 1985) whose "generic" strategies (1980: 34) include differentiation of products relative to the needs of consumers. In addition, individual producers can offer a range of products which are targeted to multiple niches.

Chamberlin (1951) provides an excellent account of the heterogeneous supply and demand perspective. He proposes that markets are characterized by spatial competition whereby buyers (each with unique demand attributes) are unevenly distributed over product space. Concentrations of populations (analogous to the groups of consumers and associated multiple demand curves suggested above) exist around certain products as a result of common tastes for certain attributes. The concept of product (or economic) space represents an analogy to literal space whereby producers of, and customers for, a homogeneous product are distributed geographically. The following comments by Chamberlin exemplify his perspective on heterogeneity of demand and supply:

> But we now have to take into account that there is actually a great diversity of products, with each seller producing a product or products of his own, different in some degree from those of others (1951: 346).

> We may speak of economic space instead of literal space, and conceive of buyers distributed symbolically throughout a multi-dimensional area containing all of the

various aspects of products (in addition to convenience)
which have already been mentioned. In the same way as
with literal space, producers are distributed throughout such
an area, and although their products may be alike in some
respects, they remain different in others (1951: 347).

The implications of spatial competition is that producers have
some degree of "local" monopoly while still being subject to
competition based upon other producers which are close to the producer
in product space. Thus Chamberlin suggests the term, "monopolistic
competition" (1951: 347). Competition is relevant due to the cross-
elasticity of alternative products which exist near the producers' own
offerings.

The concept of strategic groups in the strategic management
literature is parallel to Chamberlin's ideas on heterogeneous demand and
heterogeneous supply. Strategic groups are groupings of organizations
within an industry which pursue similar strategies with similar resources
(Hatten & Hatten, 1987). Much of the basis for strategic group research
rests on the premise espoused by Chamberlin (1951) as well as earlier
work by Triffin (1939) which suggests that the concept of industries is
inconsistent with the reality of product differentiation (McGee, 1985).
To the extent that market groupings determine strategic groups within
the industry, the concept of strategic groups is directly parallel to the
ideas about niches presented above. The implication is that groupings
of intra-industry customers will be served by correspondent groups of
firms (strategic groups). Hatten and Hatten (1987) exemplify this
perspective when they argue that groups correspond to niches within the
industry. ". . . . We can usefully talk about (strategic) groups or we can
talk about niches, the market spaces groups occupy (1987: 336)."

Perfect information. Economic models of pure competition
generally assume that consumers and producers have access to complete
information (Maurice & Smithson, 1985). Producers are assumed to
have information on the market demand curve, as well as complete
knowledge of production technologies. The outcome of complete
information on the demand curve is that no single firm can gain an
advantage through earlier or better identification of demand
characteristics. The implication of the assumption of perfect knowledge
of production technologies is that no firm can sustain a cost advantage
nor acquire economic profits relative to other industry members.
Removing the condition of perfect information allows certain firms or
individuals to have superior knowledge of markets, technologies, or

sources of supply. Consequently, economic profits become possible, and a role for the entrepreneur (seizing profit opportunities) emerges.

Dynamic versus static perspectives. Finally, neoclassical models tend to emphasize the equilibrium state of markets while ignoring, or at least minimizing, the processes which underlie movement toward, or away from, equilibrium (Kirzner, 1973). The typical approach assumes that equilibrium occurs quickly and efficiently. The assumption of perfect information of demand and supply allows the equilibrating process to occur with little friction. For example, consumers can instantly react to changes in product price which result from more efficient production technologies. Similarly, producers can rapidly imitate the technological advances of other firms, thereby bringing price down to marginal cost. As a result, there is no need to emphasize the process of market correction or the dynamics thereof.

In reality, however, the dynamics of markets are as important, if not more important, than the state of equilibrium (Kirzner, 1973). The degree of friction present in the market mechanism is important to understanding the persistence of economic profits, and the phenomenon of entrepreneurship. An emphasis on the process of disequilibration and equilibration helps to explicate the workings of the market mechanism and the subsequent effect on prices, profits, and entrepreneurship.

The fundamental issue of interest in the present research is whether models of disequilibrium provide a foundation for a better explanation of entrepreneurship and new venture formation. A review of conceptualizations of disequilibrium and entrepreneurship follows.

Theories of Disequilibrium and Entrepreneurship

The following paragraphs review and define the theoretical approaches of authors who have written about the role of the entrepreneur in markets which do not fit the neoclassical ideal. Some of the writings are of the Austrian economics tradition, while others have emanated from slightly more traditional approaches. Generally speaking, the cited authors reject the idea that entrepreneurship can be understood through general equilibrium models and therefore find it necessary to consider markets without the use of the traditional assumptions of economic analysis. An overview of each author's perspective is presented below. First, the ideas of Austrian economists Kirzner, Mises, and Rizzo are presented. Then, Leibenstein's thoughts on X-inefficiency, imperfect markets, and entrepreneurship are summarized. The classic works of Knight and Schumpeter are presented next, followed by a review of the writings of Rosen, Penrose, and Schultz. Finally, a number of perspectives from strategic management are discussed. These reviews are followed by a summary section which discusses commonalities between the perspectives.

Kirzner. The writings of Kirzner (1973, 1979, 1983) represent the codification of the Austrian economists' views of the operation of markets. Typical, or perhaps definitive, of the Austrian tradition, Kirzner focuses on the market process rather than on market equilibrium. The theory investigates how changes in the market initiate further market alterations and reactions from economic actors. Market dynamics create a state of disequilibrium whereby opportunities exist for economic actors to earn economic profits. To Kirzner, this profit opportunity is a sort of arbitrage condition whereby a given product can be purchased at a lower price than it can be sold. In addition, the arbitrage opportunities available at disequilibrium are not immediately realized by most market participants.

> A state of market disequilibrium is characterized by widespread ignorance. Market participants are unaware of the real opportunities for beneficial exchange which are available to them in the market (Kirzner, 1973: 69).

The ability of individual market participants to make timely corrections to market changes is argued to be a function of their "alertness" to the implications of such changes. Those with superior information on market changes will recognize existing opportunities and move to buy at low prices and sell at high prices. The function of the entrepreneur is to recognize the market opportunities which exist in the market place. As such, the primary entrepreneurial characteristic is alertness to such opportunity. The "pure" entrepreneur is defined by the action of identifying and seizing opportunities for profit within the economic system. The producer plays the role of both pure entrepreneur and resource owner.

The following quote from Kirzner (1979: 149) summarizes his perspective on the market process:

> What is of importance is that as the result both of the ignorance existing in the market at any given point in time, and of the circumstances that spontaneous and continual changes (in human tastes, resource availabilities, and technological knowledge) generate a ceaseless flow of fresh ignorance, as it were, into the market—that as a result of this, there is continual scope for the discovery by alert entrepreneurs of newly created opportunities. The market

offers incentives for the discovery of errors, in the profit opportunities that errors engender. Such profit opportunities rest, in the last analysis, on the circumstance, due to error, it may be the case that the current utilization of a unit of a resource or commodity fails to exploit its full productive or value potential.

According to Kirzner, as entrepreneurs recognize and act upon market opportunities, *they move the market towards equilibrium.* First of all, the arbitrage activity which entrepreneurs undertake is itself an equilibrating move since it leaves all market participants a little better off then they were before. In addition, as entrepreneurs take advantage of such opportunities, other producers recognize the existence of the opportunity and initiate appropriate productive activities. Once the opportunity is widely acknowledged, equilibrium is reached as producers react accordingly. "Once a profit opportunity has become obvious it no longer retains its character of a pure profit opportunity," and the market moves toward equilibrium (Kirzner, 1979: 149).

Kirzner's perspective of the market process is dependent upon the removal of two assumptions normally associated with models of general equilibrium. First, Kirzner focuses on the dynamic nature of markets. Kirzner recognizes that the underlying forces of markets change and does not assume that market participants can make spontaneous corrections to such changes. Market change is inclusive of changes in human tastes, resource availability, and technological knowledge, and is thereby considerate of both demand and supply dynamics. Moreover, Kirzner releases the assumption that market participants are perfectly informed of market conditions. Asymmetry of information is crucial to Kirzner's conception of the entrepreneurial role and the ability of the entrepreneur to earn profits.

It is interesting to note, however, that Kirzner still seems to adhere to the assumption of homogeneous demand and supply. There is no mention of product differentiation or market segmentation, and Kirzner focuses primarily on price and cost as the sole drivers of profit opportunity. In fact, Kirzner argues that product differentiation is present only because the market has yet to reach an equilibrium state. In addition, Kirzner explicitly rejects Chamberlin's viewpoint on heterogenous demand as just another variation of static equilibrium theory.

A simplistic view of Kirzner's basic arguments is shown in Figure II-1 below.

Fig. II-1: Kirzner's Model of Entrepreneurship

Mises. In a seminal work of the Austrian tradition, Mises (1949) describes his view on market change and the subsequent role of the entrepreneur. Since much of Kirzner's theory was built on the work of Mises, it is not surprising that the two perspectives are quite similar. Therefore, the following description of Mises's work will be brief. Mises believes that the market process tends toward equilibrium, but is interrupted when changes in the market occur. "In a changing economy there prevails always an inherent tendency for profits and losses to disappear. It is only the emergence of new changes which revives them again" (Mises, 1949: 297). As a result, entrepreneurship, and the potential for profit are "always a phenomenon of a deviation from 'normalcy' of changes unforeseen by the majority and of a 'disequilibrium'" (Mises, 1949: 297). Mises sees changes in the market as the origin of disequilibrium, and the entrepreneur as reacting to market opportunities inherent in the state of disequilibrium. In addition, Mises argues that entrepreneurial profit emanated from the bearing of uncertainty as it relates to changes in the market. The successful entrepreneur is able to correctly anticipate future relevant events. If all market participants are able to predict changes, no profit would ensue.

> Only those entrepreneurs, who, in their planning have correctly anticipated the future state of the market are in a position to reap, in selling products, an excess over the costs of production expended (Mises, 1949: 534).

In this respect, Mises agrees with the central conceptualization of the entrepreneur as proposed by Knight (1921).

A summary model of Mises' perspective on disequilibrium would look very similar to that of Kirzner, as shown in Figure II-1 above. The ideas of another Austrian economist, Mario Rizzo, are discussed below.

Rizzo. Rizzo (1979) presents some interesting arguments on the concept of disequilibrium. He emphasizes the role that time plays in causing conditions of disequilibrium. In short, Rizzo argues that disequilibrium results from the surprise and disappointment that are associated with the passage of time. In this respect, Rizzo approximates

Knight (1921) in that he gives uncertainty a prominent role. And, like Kirzner (1973), Rizzo assumes that the market for information is imperfect, and that entrepreneurial profit is dependent upon superior information. The following summarizes Rizzo's perspective.

> Disequilibrium implies that opportunities for mutually advantageous exchange exist, and that those who possess superior information will reap a kind of arbitrage profit by seizing these opportunities. Yet to seize these opportunities requires that the entrepreneur have expectations that turn out to be correct (Rizzo, 1979: 2)

Figure II-2 provides a simplified diagram of Rizzo's framework.

Fig. II-2: Rizzo's Conceptualization of Disequilibrium and Entrepreneurship

Leibenstein. Although not of the Austrian tradition, Leibenstein's concept of X-inefficiency (1966, 1968, 1979) has direct implications for a theory of entrepreneurship. Leibenstein attends primarily to the production function side of the market as it relates to disequilibrium and entrepreneurship.

Leibenstein's X-inefficiency theory (1966, 1968, 1979) argues that individuals are not maximizers and are constrained in taking advantage of available opportunities. X-inefficiency is characterized by the use of inefficient production techniques which increase costs above the optimal level. As a result of individual inertia and X-inefficiency, "firms operate under a considerable degree of slack," (Leibenstein, 1968: 75) and gaps in the market will exist which represent profit opportunities.

The existence of such profit opportunities, as in Kirzner's system, defines a state of market disequilibrium. Markets which contain such opportunities are termed "imperfect." (The term, "imperfect" will not be used beyond the present discussion due to possible confusion with its reference to imperfect market structures as referred to by terms such as monopoly and oligopoly).

The entrepreneur, in Leibenstein's theory, ferrets out opportunities in markets. Entrepreneurship is seen as the opposing force of X-inefficiency, whereby the entrepreneur is filling in market deficiencies. "Persistent slack implies the existence of entrepreneurial activities" (Leibenstein, 1968: 75). Entrepreneurship is thereby defined as:

> Activities necessary to create or carry on an enterprise where not all markets are well established or clearly defined and/or in which relevant parts of the production function are not completely known (Leibenstein, 1968: 73).

In addition, the greater the existence of X-inefficiency, the greater the potential for entrepreneurial activity.

> . . . the greater the imperfections, the wider the scope of entrepreneurial activities, and vice versa. This fits the notion that under a perfectly competitive equilibrium, the scope for entrepreneurial activities falls to zero, whereas as imperfections increase so does entrepreneurial scope. This is not to imply that there are always entrepreneurs around to meet the challenges of whatever imperfections exist." (Leibenstein, 1979: 135)

Given "imperfect" markets, Leibenstein argues that three classes of entrepreneurial activity exist: gap filling, input completing, and uncertainty bearing. Gap filling involves filling up holes in the input markets, thus overcoming the imperfections associated with inefficient markets. Input completing involves being able to fill enough gaps such that all inputs can be marshalled to produce the product or service. In other words, the entrepreneur must be able to garner all the inputs necessary for production, not just the ones which are being overlooked by inefficient producers. Uncertainty bearing refers to the fact that the entrepreneur bears some ex-ante uncertainty regarding the validity of his gap filling attempts.

Leibenstein's theorem implicitly recognizes that markets are characterized by incomplete information in addition to incomplete ability (or desire) of market participants to be efficient. Thus, Leibenstein arrives at the possibility of disequilibrium and market opportunity through the inefficiency of producers rather than through changes in either demand or supply-related market conditions. He does not directly address the dynamic changes occurring in markets. Such changes would nonetheless fit quite nicely with his arguments. Changes not adapted to by X-inefficient participants would also represent opportunities for entrepreneurs. Leibenstein also does not examine the implications of heterogeneous demand within his framework.

Fig. II-3: Leibenstein's X-Inefficiency
and Entrepreneurship

Knight. Knight (1921) provides one of the classic explanations of the function of the entrepreneur. As did Kirzner, Knight recognizes the dynamic nature of markets and the reality of imperfect information regarding market changes. In Knight's economic world, markets are continually undergoing dynamic change. According to Knight, the source of dynamic changes in markets include improved methods of production, changes in forms of organization, multiplication of consumer wants, increases in population, and increases in capital. Dynamic changes within the industry represent profit opportunities for entrepreneurs only under the condition that the change is unpredictable. Knight argues that conditions of predictable change or risk do not produce market opportunities because firms are able to plan for the consequent change. Thus, it is the uncertainty associated with change that is important to describing the profit opportunities and the extent of entrepreneurship. "Dynamic changes give rise to a peculiar form of income only insofar as the changes and their consequences are unpredictable in character" (Knight, 1921: 37). This view can be summarized by saying that Knight views change as a necessary but not sufficient condition for profit. Uncertain change gives rise to profit opportunities and entrepreneurial activity. As a result of this approach to market dynamics, Knight is well known for describing the entrepreneur as the bearer of uncertainty. Entrepreneurial profit, accordingly, is said to be a function of the entrepreneur's accuracy in predicting change, as well as the total supply of entrepreneurs.

Knight provides a theoretical basis for entrepreneurship by emphasizing the importance of changes in the industry to market opportunities for entrepreneurs. He proposes a link between change, market opportunity, and entrepreneurship. However, change, to Knight, is not the creator of opportunity unless it is *uncertain* change.

As with the other concepts and models discussed above, heterogeneous demand is not explicitly included in Knight's conceptualization. Obviously dynamic markets with imperfect information are central to Knight's theory. Knight's analysis of market change is inclusive of both demand- and supply-related dynamics. A summary diagram of Knight's theory is shown below in Figure II-4.

Fig. II-4: Knight's Conception
of Entrepreneurship

Schumpeter.   Although Schumpeter's (1934) view of entrepreneurship is widely known, it is rather different from Austrian and other perspectives discussed herein.   Schumpeter views the entrepreneur as the great *disequilibrator.* That is, Schumpeter sees the entrepreneur as the initiator of creative destruction of the circular flow of economic life. Rather than reacting to changes in the market, the entrepreneur is the creator of change. The dynamics initiated by the entrepreneur push the market into a state of disequilibrium.

> It is spontaneous and discontinuous change in the channels of flow, disturbance of equilibrium, which forever alters and displaces the equilibrium state previously existing (Schumpeter, 1934: 65).

To Schumpeter, the entrepreneur is the innovator who implements change within markets through the carrying out of new combinations. Carrying out new combinations can take any of five forms: 1) the introduction of a new good or quality thereof, 2) the introduction of a new method of production, 3) the opening of a new market, 4) the conquest of a new source of supply of new materials or parts, or 5) the carrying out of the new organization of any industry (Schumpeter, 1934: 66). A model of the Schumpeterian view is shown in Figure II-5 below.

Schumpeter's approach to markets obviously treats their dynamic nature. In addition, his model implicitly assumes imperfect information. Otherwise, the entrepreneurial profits about which Schumpeter speaks would not be possible. The new combinations Schumpeter discusses would be equally available to all firms if perfect information were assumed. Schumpeter also does not preclude the possibility of heterogeneous supply and demand from his analysis. One of the possibilities for new combinations is variation in products or product quality. As such, Schumpeter recognizes the fact that producers can serve demand through the modification of product attributes.

Rosen. Rosen's (1983) work on the economics of entrepreneurship is directly parallel to that of the Austrian perspective. Similar to the other authors discussed above, Rosen sees a role for entrepreneurship only in markets which are "incomplete."

> I therefore conclude that in the presence of complete markets in all transactions (which in itself implies a the kind of complete information), there is no role for entrepreneur to play, no scope for the entrepreneur at all (Rosen, 1983: 303)

Fig. II-5: Schumpeter's Creative Destruction

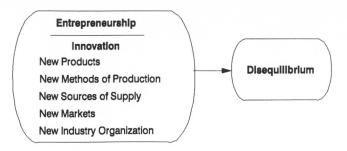

But Rosen argues that many markets are not complete, and the entrepreneur therefore has a role to play. Some markets do not exist because they are too small, and some are incomplete because the available transactions change over time. He identified two types of possible change in markets. "Normal changes," such as changes in income and factor supplies, merely call forth reallocations of existing transactions. Other, "non-routine changes," bring the creation of new markets, new goods and services, and new ways of doing things. Non-routine changes represent opportunities for entrepreneurial activity.

> In a steady state with unchanging conditions, the amount of entrepreneurship would tend to a limit of zero. . . . A sustained rate of entrepreneurial activity occurs in a society that is constantly in a state of flux, forever changing (Rosen, 1983: 307).

Another interesting aspect of Rosen's work is his consideration of the difference between invention and entrepreneurship. Rosen considers the two activities quite distinct.

> . . . Entrepreneurship is not invention. Rather it is exploiting the new opportunities that inventors provide, more in the form of marketing and developing them for widespread use in the economy than developing the knowledge itself (Rosen, 1983: 307).

This is parallel to the ideas presented by the Austrian economists, and is central to their rejection of the Schumpeterian (1934) perspective on entrepreneurship as a disequilibrating force. Invention creates the situation of disequilibrium, entrepreneurship moves it back towards a new equilibrium. "To that extent, one might say that invention is the mother of entrepreneurship" (Rosen, 1983: 307). Rosen's conceptualization of entrepreneurship is shown in Figure II-6.

Fig. II-6: Rosen's Conceptualization
of Entrepreneurship

Penrose. Edith Penrose's treatment (1963) differs from the others presented above in that she is mainly concerned with the growth of the firm, rather than with economic growth or entrepreneurship. She attempts to explain why certain firms grow while others do not. However, central to her thesis on firm growth is entrepreneurship. Entrepreneurial activity involves identifying opportunities in the market, and "the rate and direction of the growth of a firm depends on the extent to which it is alert to act upon opportunities for profitable investment" (Penrose, 1963:30). Thus, the function of the entrepreneur is to identify opportunities within the economic system. Entrepreneurs can exist within a firm, or can be associated with the creation of a new firm.

For the most part, Penrose argues that incumbent firms will always have an advantage over new entrants in identifying and acting upon available market opportunities. However, in a growing economy, Penrose admits the greater potential for small and new-firm entrepreneurship. A growing economy results from population growth, technological advance, development of new resources or industries, shifts in consumer tastes and preferences, and the expansion of consumer wants. If the incumbent firms are unable to keep up with the rate of growth in the economy, and they are unable to preclude new entrants from operating in an industry, entrant entrepreneurs can arise.

> If, therefore, the opportunities for expansion in the economy increase at a faster rate than the large firms can take advantage of them, and if the large firms cannot prevent the entry of small firms, there will be scope for continued growth in the size and number of favorably endowed small firms . . . . (Penrose, 1963: 222).

Penrose terms such opportunities for small firms (including new entrants), "interstices in the economy" (Penrose, 1963: 223) Large firms unable to take advantage of all profitable opportunities will take the most profitable ones and leave the remainder as interstices for small and entrant firms. However, interstices otherwise available to entrants will be eliminated if firms are able to erect barriers to entry.

> The ability of small firms to seize on profitable opportunities in which they can grow will be destroyed if barriers are erected against their entry . . . . (Penrose, 1963: 228).

In summary, Penrose sees entrepreneurial activity as motivated by opportunities that exist within the economic system. New firm entrepreneurs will be able to seize such opportunities only if large firms are too slow to take advantage of all the opportunities available to them, and if no barriers to entry are erected against them.

A summary of Penrose's model of entrepreneurship and small firm (including new entrants) entrepreneurship is provided below.

Schultz. Schultz (1975) discusses the value of an individual's ability to perceive disequilibria, and if appropriate, to reallocate his/her resources accordingly. According to Schultz, disequilibrium is a result of a variety of events which occur within a given market. The demand for entrepreneurial ability is a function of the presence of a state of disequilibrium, and the nature thereof. At disequilibrium, economic

Fig. II-7: Penrose, and Large and Small
Firm Entrepreneurship

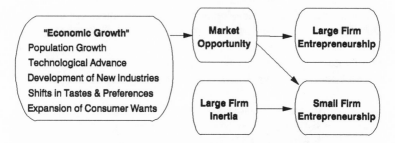

to such incentives, but the ability of individuals to recognize incentives and reallocate resources varies. Thus, entrepreneurial talent is hypothesized to be central to an individual's ability to earn profits in a changing world. Entrepreneurial ability

> . . . represents the competence of people to perceive a given disequilibrium and to evaluate its attributes properly in determining whether it is worthwhile to act, and if it is worthwhile, people respond by re-allocating their resources (Schultz, 1975: 834).

Schultz provides an interesting link between education (a partial determinant of an individual's ability to deal with disequilibria) and the adoption of agricultural technologies. He argues that adopters of agricultural technologies are entrepreneurs reallocating their resources in response to opportunities created by change, and that the rate of reallocation will be higher, the greater the level of education of the population.

Strategic management perspectives: Porter, Yip, and Sandberg. Although discussions of disequilibrium have been rare in the strategic management literature, three authors have considered the subject. Porter (1980) argues that a state of industry disequilibrium implies that the market mechanism is not working perfectly and that industries in disequilibrium contain special opportunities for potential entrants which may allow them to overcome high entry barriers. According to Porter, three types of industries can be classified as being at disequilibrium. The first type occurs when the industry is new and its competitive structure is not yet well established. The second type occurs when entry barriers are increasing over time, and the new entrant can gain a foothold before the doors close. The third type is where there is imperfect information regarding the cost of entry and expected profits. Thus a lack of recognition of opportunities by other firms creates a situation whereby a new entrant can gain advantage.

Yip (1982) expands upon and empirically tests Porter's thoughts on disequilibrium and entry. Using the PIMS database, Yip tests the effect of entry barriers, entry inducements, strategic heterogeneity, and industry disequilibrium on a dichotomous measure of industry entry. Like Porter, Yip proposes that a state of industry disequilibrium eases the entry of firms into an industry. He views disequilibrium somewhat narrowly as the condition of temporary excess demand, and proposed rapid industry growth rate, high-capacity utilization, recent technological change, and recent exit as indicators of disequilibrium. Overall, the disequilibrium variables used by Yip support the link between disequilibrium and entry. Market growth is highly positively related to entry. Exit also has a significant impact on entry. Contrary to his hypothesis, capacity utilization has a negative effect on entry. Both technological change and new product development activity are significantly positively related to entry when tested independently of each other.

Sandberg (1986) performs an extensive study of the causes of new venture performance. Using Austrian economic viewpoints, he suggests that the performance of new ventures will be greater for ventures started in markets which are at disequilibrium. Using industry life-cycle stages as a proxy measure of disequilibrium, Sandberg finds that entrants to developing or growth industries fare better than entrants to latter-stage industries. Using a measure of "evident disequilibrium," Sandberg again shows that entrants to markets in disequilibrium have higher performance.

Figure II-8 below shows the model of equilibrium and entry suggested by Yip and later adopted by Sandberg.

Fig. II-8: Sandberg and Yip's Models
of Disequilibrium and Entrepreneurship

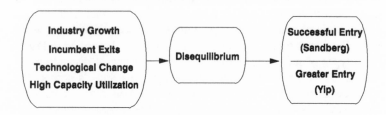

Summary of Disequilibrium Theories

The foregoing review presented the work of a number of authors who have discussed the role of market disequilibrium and entrepreneurship. The authors work in a variety of disciplines, including industrial organization economics, Austrian economics, and strategic management. It is illuminating that these writings come from such a wide array of perspectives, yet arrive at a number of similar theoretical propositions. The major points of each of the authors is summarized in Table II-1. The following discussion will highlight the primary points of these authors as related to the topic of entrepreneurship.

Discussion and integration of disequilibrium theories of entrepreneurship. The relationship between a state of market disequilibrium and the presence of market opportunities is a common theme discussed by most of the 11 cited authors. The central idea is that market opportunities are inherent in a state of disequilibrium. To the Austrian economists (Kirzner, 1973; Mises, 1949; Rizzo, 1979), the concept of disequilibrium is the foundation of theoretical propositions on the dynamics of markets. Rosen (1983) describes the existence of incomplete markets and discusses opportunities available in such markets. Similarly, Leibenstein's concept of X-inefficient markets is directly parallel to the idea of disequilibrium. Porter (1980) argues that markets at equilibrium would not be attractive to firms, but those in a state of disequilibrium could be successfully entered. Again, the common theme is that a state of disequilibrium presents opportunities to economic actors. This idea is so pervasive that one might consider

TABLE II-1: SUMMARY OF THEORETICAL ARGUMENTS ON ENTREPRENEURSHIP

Kirzner (1973, 1979, 1983)

Market change and widespread ignorance of change create state of disequilibrium.
Alert entrepreneurs move toward opportunities at disequilibrium and thereby earn profit.
Entrepreneurship moves market towards equilibrium.

Mises (1949)

Changes in markets unforeseen by the majority of participants result in disequilibrium.
Entrepreneurs react to market opportunity inherent in a state of disequilibrium.
Profit emanates from the bearing of uncertainty.

Rizzo (1979)

The passage of time results in uncertainty and market disequilibrium.
Profit will be available to those with superior information.

Leibenstein (1966, 1968, 1979)

Non-maximizing behavior and inertia in individual action results in organizational entropy
(X-inefficiency).
Market gaps created by X-inefficiency are sought out by entrepreneurs.
Entrepreneurship involves gap filling, input completing, and uncertainty bearing.

Knight (1921)

Dynamic, unpredictable changes in markets represent opportunities for entrepreneurs.
Entrepreneurship involves the bearing of uncertainty.
Change is a necessary but not sufficient condition for profit.

Schumpeter (1934)

The entrepreneur is an innovator who creates change through carrying out new
combinations.
The entrepreneur disturbs market equilibrium and moves it into disequilibrium.

Rosen (1983)

Non-routine changes in markets represent opportunities for entrepreneurial activity.
Entrepreneurship occurs only in incomplete markets.

Penrose (1963)

Entrepreneurship involves identifying opportunities in the organizational environment.
If incumbent firms can't keep up with emerging opportunities and are unable to preclude
entrants, new entrant entrepreneurs can move toward the opportunities.

Schultz (1975)

Entrepreneurial activity is a function of the existence of disequilibrium.

Porter (1980)

Industries in a state of disequilibrium represent opportunities for potential entrants.

Yip (1982)/Sandberg (1986)

Disequilibrium results from or is indicated by industry growth, incumbent exits,
technological change, and high capacity utilization.
Entry will be increased and will be more successful when a market is at disequilibrium.

disequilibrium to be defined by the presence of opportunity. In other words, it may be appropriate to define a state of disequilibrium by the existence of profit opportunities.

Moreover, disequilibrium implies entrepreneurship. It is argued that the function of the entrepreneur is to move towards market opportunities which are available at disequilibrium. The role of the entrepreneur is to react to market opportunities and thereby earn economic profits (Kirzner, 1973; Mises, 1949). According to Leibenstein (1979), market gaps existing in X-inefficient markets are sought out by entrepreneurs who perform the functions of gap filling, input completing, and uncertainty bearing. Rosen (1983) suggests that entrepreneurship occurs only in incomplete markets and Schultz (1975) argues that entrepreneurs perceive disequilibrium and reallocate resources accordingly. To Kirzner (1973), the entrepreneurial act of exploiting market opportunities moves the market toward equilibrium. Thus, taking advantage of opportunities fills the gaps in markets, makes them more complete, and moves them to a more efficient state.

The disequilibrium literature is also concerned with the factors which create disequilibria. A common theme in these writings is that the dynamics of industries cause a state of disequilibrium. Most of the authors would agree that markets tend toward equilibrium. Therefore, under stable conditions, it is likely that the market would equilibrate. However, when changes occur, markets move away from a state of equilibrium, and opportunities are created. According to Kirzner (1979), changes in factors such as human tastes, resource availability, and technological knowledge create a flow of new opportunities for alert entrepreneurs to exploit. To Mises (1949), changes which are unforeseen by the majority of market participants revive the potential for profits and entrepreneurship. This view is also espoused by Knight (1921), as long as the market dynamics are unpredictable in nature. Similarly, Rosen suggests that non-routine changes are responsible for the creation of entrepreneurial opportunity. Rizzo (1979) emphasizes the role of the passage of time in bringing forth the changes which create disequilibrium.

Central to a valid linkage between market opportunities, entrepreneurship, and the ability to earn economic profit is the concept that not all economic actors move toward opportunities. Part of this theory results from the existence of imperfect information. According to Knight (1921), predictable market change does not create opportunities since market actors would quickly move to alleviate any profit potential of the relevant changes. Market opportunities are created only when dynamics are not evident to market participants. As a result, Knight emphasizes the role of the entrepreneur in bearing uncertainty. Kirzner (1973), Mises (1949), and Rizzo (1979) emphasize the fact that entrepreneurs need to be more alert and possess superior information on market conditions and the implications of changes. "Widespread ignorance" (Kirzner, 1973: 69) of market conditions is what allows dynamically created profit opportunities to persist. In other words, the asymmetrical nature of market information is what allows the entrepreneurial role to emerge. In addition, the persistence of a state of disequilibrium may result from incumbent firms not moving towards opportunities, even though the incumbents know of the existence of opportunities. Penrose suggests that existing firms may not be able to keep up with all of the changes occurring in a highly dynamic situation. Thus, profit opportunities will be left for new entrants. Leibenstein (1979) even suggests that the inertial properties of X-inefficient firms is what creates the market gaps in the first place. At any rate, both incomplete (or nonexistent) information and the failure of some firms to react to market dynamics and disequilibria results in profit opportunities that persist. The persistence of profit opportunities encourages entrepreneurship and the creation of new businesses.

The following provides a summary viewpoint of how these authors might agree on the nature of markets and entrepreneurship. Dynamic, unpredictable changes in markets create a state of disequilibrium. This disequilibrium persists due to the existence of information asymmetries, and inertial (X-inefficient) properties of individuals and firms. Economic actors with superior alertness to changes and the state of disequilibrium move to exploit opportunities and earn economic profits. Thus, the role of the entrepreneur is to discover and seize market opportunities through the reallocation of productive resources. As the entrepreneur performs these activities, the market is moved closer to a state of equilibrium. Dynamic change is a disequilibrating force that is constantly reacted to by the equilibrating action of entrepreneurship.

As alluded to above, the conceptualization of the entrepreneur espoused by most of the authors reviewed herein does not neatly fit within the Schumpeterian (1934) perspective of entrepreneurship. The Schumpeterian theory of entrepreneurship and economic development is both similar, and counter, to the ideas discussed above. It is similar in the respect that entrepreneurship is seen as a dominant force in economic development, and in the evolution of markets. However, Schumpeter views the entrepreneurial process as a disequilibrating force, while Austrian theory and the discussion of many of the other cited authors suggests that entrepreneurship acts to equilibrate the market.

Cheah (1990) provides an interesting comparison of Schumpeterian and Austrian views. Cheah suggests that both Schumpeterian and Austrian entrepreneurial types exist and that the Schumpeterian entrepreneur creates the disequilibrium which the Austrian entrepreneur can subsequently act upon. The ideas of Cheah regarding a reconciliation between Schumpeterian and Austrian perspective on entrepreneurship will be explored and further developed in the next chapter.

In the above discussion, two major points need further elaboration. The first is that the dynamics of industries create profit opportunities and encourage entrepreneurship. If industry changes encourage entrepreneurship, it is also likely that industry change will motivate the creation of new firms. The second point is that existing firms may be inertial or X-inefficient regarding opportunities available in a market. If existing firms are inertial and thereby do not move to opportunities, new venture creation may increase accordingly. The next two sections address these points. First, a discussion of the meaning of industry change is presented. In addition, studies which have looked at a relation between industry dynamics and new venture creation are reviewed. Then, the role of organizational inertia in the creation of new ventures is presented.

INDUSTRY DYNAMICS

The above discussion points to a relationship between the dynamics of industries, the market opportunities available in an industry, entrepreneurship, and new venture formation. Therefore, it is important to further explicate the meaning of industry dynamism. In the following discussion, conceptualizations of dynamism are reviewed. First, economic viewpoints are presented. These viewpoints are useful for understanding the sources of change in an industry environment. Then, the concept of dynamism is examined from the perspective of organization theorists and others. Organizational researchers provide excellent discussions on the nature of the total environment which organizations face. The more specific industry environment can be viewed as an important part of the total organizational environment (see, for example, Hrebiniak & Snow, 1980). The review will lead into a discussion of the role of existing firm inertia in encouraging entrepreneurship and new business formations.

Economic Perspectives on Industry Dynamics

Industry change refers to the alteration of the market's fundamental conditions of demand and supply (Knight, 1921; Marshall, 1890) and can take several forms. Put in terms of popular comparative statics analysis, industry change can be seen as any factor which might result in a shift in the demand or supply curve. Among the exogenous variables which economists believe impact the demand curve are the incomes of consumers, prices of related commodities, consumer tastes and preferences, and expectations about future prices (Maurice & Smithson, 1985). The level of technology, prices of inputs, and future expectations about the price of the commodity are usually associated with shifts in the supply curve (Maurice & Smithson, 1985). Assuming heterogeneous demand, dynamics other than a simple shift in a single demand or supply curve can occur within an industry. For example, shifts in consumer tastes and preferences can increase one sub-industry level demand (niche) while decreasing another. Changing technology can completely eliminate one niche and/or create another.

A number of economists have discussed the specific sources of industry change and the dynamics of markets. The sources suggested by each of these authors are discussed below.

Schumpeter (1934) was concerned with changes in the circular flow of economic life that disturb the prior state of equilibrium. His conceptualization of change specifically excludes modifications of consumer wants and needs and focuses on the production side of alterations in markets. In addition, Schumpeter excludes changes which arise from continuous improvements. His conceptualization of change focuses entirely on discontinuous modifications to productive means. These discontinuous modifications are viewed as new combinations of productive means and are inclusive of five cases: the introduction of new products, the introduction of new methods of production, the development of new sources of supply, the opening of new markets, and the carrying out of a new industry organization.

Kirzner (1973) discusses the factors necessary in order for the market process to continue beyond a state of equilibrium. These autonomous changes include changes in human tastes, resource availability, and technological knowledge. Such changes create the potential for entrepreneurs to alter the pattern of market opportunity and thereby earn profits.

Knight (1921) describes generic types of dynamic change: increasing population, increasing capital, improving methods of production, multiplication of consumer wants, and changes in the forms of industrial establishments. These dynamic changes alter the social structure and are argued to be the exclusive creators of profit.

Penrose (1963) identifies a number of forces that act to stimulate the growth of an economy, and subsequently, the growth of the firm. These forces create interstices in the economy and include population growth, technological advance leading to the development of new resources and of new industries, shifts in consumers' tastes, expansion of consumer wants, and increased savings and capital accumulation.

Finally, Rosen (1983) discusses the non-routine changes which create incomplete markets and give rise to entrepreneurial activities. Non-routine changes are inclusive of the creation of new markets, new goods, new services, and new ways of doing things. Non-routine changes are not inclusive of normal changes such as changes in income, factor supplies, and others that call forth reallocations within existing markets.

Organization theorists have discussed environmental change and market dynamics for more than 30 years. The discussion of these viewpoints will enhance understanding of the meaning of market dynamics.

Organization Theory Perspectives on Environmental Dynamics

Early in the history of the study of organizations, researchers gave little concern to the role of the environment in determining organizational structure and operation (Miles, Snow, & Pfeffer, 1974). However, after disillusionment with the universalistic principles of bureaucratic management, researchers became interested in the role of the organizational environment (Miles et. al., 1974). Burns and Stalker (1961) for example, suggest that mechanistic and organic forms of organization are appropriate to different organizational environments. In addition, the conceptualization of organizations as open systems (Katz & Kahn, 1966) provides the theoretical foundation upon which the importance of the environment could be investigated. Research on organizational environments has led to a number of definitions and descriptions of organizational environments, as well as a number of perspectives on the role of the environment in determining organizational structures and strategies. *Definitions and conceptualizations of organizational environments are useful to our understanding of how dynamics might relate to new venture formations.* In addition, some of the perspectives espoused by organizational researchers have implications for explaining new business creations. Contrary to the ideas of economics researchers who discuss the sources of change or types of change agents, organization researchers look at the nature of change.

The concept of organizational environment has been broadly conceived by organization researchers. In a review of research on organizational environments, Starbuck (1983) lists 20 terms that have been used to describe organizational environments. Fortunately, researchers have made the concept of environment much more specific by discussing various dimensions thereof. One rough classification is that of direct-action versus indirect-action environments (Elbing, 1974). The direct-action environment includes all factors outside the organization's boundaries that directly impact the organization's activities. Elements of the direct-action environment include the organization's customers, suppliers, employees, competitors, and government regulatory agencies. The indirect-action environment affects the climate in which the organization exists and includes the economic, political, and social situation of the organization.

One of the first specific classifications of environments is by Emery and Trist (1965). These authors discuss the difference between placid-randomized, placid-clustered, disturbed-reactive, and turbulent field environments. Terreberry (1968) further discusses the idea of turbulent field environments and argues that their primary characteristic is uncertainty. Thompson (1967) argues that environments could be classified according to a homogeneous/heterogeneous dimension, and a stable/shifting dimension. Similarly, Lawrence and Lorsch (1967) use diversity and dynamism dimensions to capture the nature of organizational environments. Child (1972) discusses the dimensions of environmental complexity, illiberality, and variability. A useful summary list of environmental dimensions was proposed by Aldrich (1979). Aldrich's environmental components include capacity, stability, heterogeneity, dispersion, turbulence, and domain consensus. Finally, Dess and Beard (1984) argue that these six dimensions can be reduced to a more parsimonious list of three, including munificence, complexity, and dynamism. Conceptually these three are parallel to those presented by Child (Dess & Beard, 1984). Munificence is similar to Aldrich's concept of environmental capacity, and can be defined as "the extent to which the environment can support the sustained growth" of an organization (Dess & Beard, 1984: 55). Environmental dynamism is concerned with changes that are difficult to predict and thereby increase the uncertainty faced by organizations (Dess & Beard, 1984). Environmental complexity takes account of the heterogeneity and extent of an organization's environment (Dess & Beard, 1984). Generally organizations which must deal with a greater number of factors in their environment face a highly complex situation. Dess & Beard argue that organizations with more complex environments will face greater uncertainty. However, Duncan (1972) provides evidence to indicate that dynamism is a more important precursor to uncertainty than complexity.

At any rate, the purpose of the present discussion is not to present a complete review of organizational researchers' conceptualizations of environments. Rather, the purpose is to further explicate the meaning of environmental dynamism and understand its link to market disequilibria and new venture formations. Thus, the following discussion looks more specifically at the concept of environmental dynamism in organizational research.

As discussed above, Dess & Beard conceptualize environmental dynamism as unpredictable change in organizational environments. Aldrich's (1979) stability-instability and turbulence dimensions are included in Dess and Beard's definition of dynamism. Stability-instability concerns the turnover of elements in the environment (Aldrich, 1979) while turbulence concerns "the extent to which environments are being disturbed by increasing environmental interconnection, and an increasing rate of interconnection" (Aldrich, 1979: 69). Turbulent environments therefore have dynamic properties which arise as a result of the extensive interconnections with other organizations and result in a high degree of uncertainty (Emery & Trist, 1965). Perhaps, though, the idea of environmental dynamism is best explicated by the discussions of Child (1972) and later empirically corroborated by Wholey and Brittain (1989). Environmental variability "refers to the degree of change which characterizes environmental activities relevant to an organization's operations" (Child, 1972: 3). Child proposes that environmental variability could be further specified by looking at "1) the frequency of changes in relevant environmental activities, 2) the degree of difference involved at each change, and 3) the degree of irregularity in the overall pattern of change-in a sense the 'variability of change'" (Child, 1972: 3). In an empirical examination of measures of environmental variation, Wholey and Brittain (1989) propose a perceptual scheme of variation which is directly parallel to that used by Child and is useful for understanding the dimensions of environmental dynamism. They suggest that environmental variation be characterized according to its frequency, amplitude, and unpredictability. The frequency and amplitude of change are similar to Child's conceptualization of the frequency and degree of difference of change. The idea of predictability is most parallel to Child's ideas on the irregularity of change.

Relation Between Economic and Organization Theory Perspectives on Dynamics

The common theme running through much of the economics research discussed in the prior section is that dynamic changes in industry environments lead to the creation of market opportunities and thereby encourage entrepreneurship and new venture formation (Kirzner, 1979; Knight, 1921; Leibenstein, 1979; Penrose, 1963 and others). One may recall that these theories also give a prominent role to the predictability of change. Knight (1921), for example, argues that only unpredictable change creates opportunities for entrepreneurs. Kirzner (1973, 1979) emphasizes the widespread ignorance which is created by industry dynamics, while Rosen (1983) suggests that only non-routine changes represent market opportunities.

The primary role given to the industry change and its unpredictability by economists is corroborated by the importance that it is given by organizational theorists and researchers. As discussed above, many organizational researchers argue that environmental dynamism and predictability thereof is of utmost importance to the management of organizations.

The central theme of many theories of organizations is that organizational success is a function of a proper fit between an organization's strategy and structure and its environment (Bedeian & Zammuto, 1991). Contingency theorists (Burns & Stalker, 1961; Emery & Trist, 1965; Terreberry, 1968), for example, hypothesize that organizational design is dependent upon the nature of environmental change. Burns and Stalker (1961) suggest that organic organizations are appropriate for changing environments, whereas mechanistic forms are appropriate for stable conditions. Terreberry (1968) argues that organizations in turbulent environments need an increased ability to adapt to environmental contingencies. Using different assumptions regarding the deterministic nature of change, strategic choice theorists contend that managers have considerable discretion in the strategy-structure responses to environmental conditions (Child, 1972; Miles, et. al., 1974; Hambrick, 1989). In addition, organizations may even be able to manipulate the environment through, for example, alterations in their resource dependencies (Pfeffer & Salancik, 1978). Population ecologists also give prominence to the relation between organization forms and environmental conditions, but in contrast to strategic choice theorists, they argue that the adaptability of organizations to the environment is limited (Hannan & Freeman, 1977). Each of the aforementioned theoretical perspectives on organizations give considerable attention to the role of environmental variation in organizational design.

While it is difficult to find organization theory research that implies that unpredictable change directly impacts new venture formations (as might be suggested by Austrian economists), important theoretical arguments exist that imply that dynamic changes encourage new venture formations when existing firms are inertial in their reactions to change. Indeed, within organization theory, the inertial properties of organizations and the impact of inertia on the potential for the creation of new firms is often discussed. The concept of inertia as it relates to new venture formations will be reviewed in the following section.

ORGANIZATIONAL INERTIA

The question of whether existing organizations can adapt to environmental variation has been a "central theoretical debate" in organization research (Astley & Van de Ven, 1983: 244). The basic issue is whether or not existing organizations are limited in their ability to recognize and act upon opportunities despite the fact that such opportunities are present in their industry.

> There is a fundamental question about whether organizations very often alter basic patterns in activity; about the extent to which they tend to persist in activity patterns even as environments change and/or as performance outcomes are low (Romanelli & Tushman 1986: 609).

Indeed, the concept of organizational inertia is so fundamental that it has been suggested and investigated by researchers from a broad and diverse set of perspectives. These perspectives include organization theory, economics, population ecology, strategic management, and others.

Early in the history of organization theory, authors recognized the deleterious consequences of bureaucracy (March & Simon, 1958;

Blau, 1956). One perspective is that bureaucracies engender dysfunctional learning behavior within organizations (March & Simon, 1958). In addition, bureaucratic forms of organization create a ritualistic orientation which makes alterations to institutional structure impossible (Blau, 1956). At its extreme such a condition creates an organizational approach whereby the organization becomes an end in itself rather than a means to achieving its initial purpose (Blau, 1956).

> Adherence to rules, originally conceived as a means, becomes transformed into an end in itself; there occurs the familiar process of displacement of goals whereby an instrumental value becomes a terminal value (Merton, 1949: 154).

As a result of the displacement of goals in a bureaucratic organization, personnel may strongly resist change (Blau, 1956). Such an organizational rigidity is problematic, "particularly when emergent problems call for a reorganization of working procedures" (Blau, 1956: 89).

Stinchcombe (1965) suggests that firms tend to become institutionalized and that the basic structure of organizations remains relatively stable throughout time. More recently, organization theorists have argued that organizations are predominantly characterized by periods of convergence (Tushman & Romanelli, 1985) and momentum (Miller & Friesen, 1980) whereby organizational change is incremental and reversals or re-directions rarely occur. Major stimuli are required for organizations to undergo periods of revolution and organizations are thereby sluggish in their ability to respond to environmental change (Miller & Friesen, 1980). Tushman and Anderson (1986) suggest that inertia may be greater when environmental change is competence destroying rather than competence enhancing.

Leibenstein argues that firms do not exhibit complete optimizing behavior (1979):

> . . . Neither individuals nor groups (say, firms) work as hard or as effectively or search for new information and techniques as diligently as they could, nor is effort maintained at a constant level (1968: 75).

Instead, organizations tend toward X-inefficiency whereby the costs of production are not always minimized. X-inefficiency results because individuals vary in the "effort position" they take in carrying out their jobs. In other words, different individuals or groups will chose different activities to carry out, and will vary in the pace and quality of effort in carrying out those activities. In addition, individuals are often inert in changing the nature of their efforts. This inertia stems from the psychological cost of moving from one "effort position" to another (Leibenstein, 1979: 130). Maximizers will have "zero inertia" in their activities, but maximization does not match reality (Leibenstein, 1979: 130). Rather, inertia is common in human action, and, as a result, firms will not always minimize the costs of production. In addition, the cumulative effects of individual non-maximization create a tendency toward "organizational entropy" whereby X-inefficiency increases up to a point (Leibenstein, 1979: 131). Organizational entropy is the constant tendency for organizations to move to an increasing state of X-inefficiency.

Population ecologists have taken the most extreme stance on the subject of organizational inertia. Hannan and Freeman (1984) argue that inertial properties are so strong that timely adaptation to environmental change is nearly impossible. "Organizations are set on a course at founding from which change may be costly or difficult" (Boeker, 1988: 51). As a result, organizations which are inappropriate to new environmental conditions will be selected out.

In sharp contrast to the population ecology perspective, strategic management researchers argue that organizations possess a high degree of strategic choice (Child, 1972; Hambrick, 1989), and are capable of adapting to environmental change as well as manipulating or enacting the environment (Astley & Van de Ven, 1983; Weick, 1977).

Recently, it seems that researchers are recognizing that organizations are both adaptive and inertial (Bedeian & Zammuto, 1991). This middle-ground perspective is evident in a recent book on evolutionary approaches to organizations (Singh, 1990). In his book, Singh argues that adaptation and selection views are complementary, and that it is time to begin examining the conditions under which the assumption of organizational inertia is valid. Indeed, the compromise perspective on organization inertia has already been partially verified by empirical studies. Miller & Friesen (1980) find that inertia (momentum) is pervasive in organizations, but that occasional revolutions (whereby a high proportion of strategic variables were reversed) do occur. Frederickson and Iaquinto (1989) find that the decision processes of firms do not change significantly over several years, thereby supporting the existence of inertia. Boeker (1989) studied the conditions under which an initial strategic direction was altered. He found examples of organizations which underwent strategic change and were not entirely inertial, but nonetheless conclude that "organizations have at least some tendency toward inertia" (Boeker, 1989: 510). Boeker's results indicate that organizations are inertial under certain conditions and that imprinting at founding constrains subsequent strategic adaptation. In sum, the evidence seems to indicate that organizations can alter their strategic direction but are often constrained by inertial processes. Furthermore, organizations vary in the inertia which they exhibit, and can be characterized accordingly. Rather than being one of two extremes, organizational inertia can be viewed as a continuum with some organizations exhibiting a higher degree of inertia than others.

The implication for the present research is that firms which are inertial will be less responsive to environmental change and will not act to exploit market and profit opportunities. When incumbent firms do not react to market opportunities, those opportunities will be available to new-firm entrants. Thus, industries which contain firms with high inertial properties are likely to exhibit greater new venture creation given the existence of market opportunities. This argument was advanced by Penrose (1963), who argues that opportunities not taken by large firms will be exploited by new or small firms. Kirzner (1979) emphasizes the role that the widespread ignorance of market participants play in allowing the continued existence of market opportunities. Leibenstein (1979) proposes that the greater the X-inefficiency within an industry, the greater the opportunities for entrepreneurs. If firms do not adequately minimize costs, opportunities will exist for non-incumbent firms. The entrepreneur is seen as making up for deficiencies in the production function which occur due to an organization's inertia in adapting the production function (Leibenstein, 1968). Yip (1982) argues that constraints on incumbent responses allow entrants to avoid or overcome entry barriers. Winter addresses the issue of inertia and venture formation as follows:

> . . . The appearance of new organizations with new forms or routines is a substitute for adaptation by existing organizations, and often plays an important role (1990: 293).

Finally, within the population ecology perspective, the inertial properties of organizations is what allows the success of new organizations with variations that more appropriately fit existing environmental conditions (Hannan & Freeman, 1984).

Ecological models of organizations have a number of implications for new venture creation and deserve further examination.

The review of ecological models in the following section explicates the role of dynamics and inertia in new venture creation, as well as describes additional implications for venture formations which result at the community/institutional level of analysis.

ECOLOGICAL MODELS OF ORGANIZATIONAL FOUNDINGS

Ecological models of organizations are particularly relevant to the study of new venture formations (Low & MacMillan, 1988; Aldrich & Wiedenmayer, 1991). Ecological models approach the study of organizations at population, and community/institutional levels of analysis, and each of these levels of analysis have implications for organizational foundings (Aldrich & Wiedenmayer, 1991).

Population Ecology

Populations are aggregates of organizations which are similar in some respect (Hannan & Freeman, 1977). More specifically, organizations within a population have a common form which is defined according to their structure, patterns of activity, or normative ways of organizing (Hannan & Freeman, 1977). The study of intra-population processes are relevant to the study of foundings in two respects.

First, researchers have examined the interdependence of foundings and failures over time, as well as their density dependence (density dependence refers to the relationship between the carrying capacity of an organizational environment and the number of organizations existing in that environment) (Aldrich & Wiedenmayer, 1991). Research on these topics is relevant to new venture formations but is somewhat out of the scope of the present research and will not be discussed herein (for an extensive discussion of these topics as they relate to organizational foundings see Aldich & Wiedenmayer, 1991).

The second area concerns what Aldrich and Wiedenmayer (1991) have termed density-independent processes. Density-independent processes are most relevant to the present study, and concern the relationship between innovation (Aldrich & Wiedenmayer, 1991) and other environmental variations (Hannan & Freeman, 1984), and organizational foundings. In the population perspective, the environment is seen as making resources available to organizations

(Aldrich, 1979). If organizations are of the appropriate form, they will be supported by environmental resources and thereby survive. Changes in the environment create problems for organizations which may or may not be appropriate to the new conditions. In short, environmental variation will require parallel variation in the form of organizations within a population. This raises the fundamental question of whether organizations can learn about environmental changes and alter their structures and strategy as quickly as the environment changes (Hannan & Freeman, 1984). If organizations cannot adapt quickly, opportunities will arise for the creation of new firms.

> One of the most important kinds of threats to the success of extant organizations is the creation of new organizations designed specifically to take advantage of some new set of opportunities. If the existing organizations cannot change their strategies or structures more quickly than entrepreneurs can begin new organizations, new competitors will have a chance to establish footholds (Hannan & Freeman, 1984: 152).

In addition, population ecologists claim that organizations are indeed subject to strong inertial forces and are limited in their ability to adapt to environmental variations. Organizational foundings are therefore seen as the source of much of the variation in organizational forms. Taking these theoretical perspectives one step further, the population ecology perspective implies that environmental variation will create resource opportunities which will draw entrepreneurs into forming new organizations.

Population ecologists have provided extensive descriptions of organizational inertia and its source. Limitations on a firm's ability to adapt can be both internal and external (Hannan & Freeman, 1977). Environmental (external) constraints on organizational action include legal and fiscal barriers to entry and exit, external constraints on information availability, legitimacy constraints, and collective rationality (Hannan & Freeman, 1977). Internal structural arrangements which generate inertia include investments in plant and equipment, information availability constraints, and organizational history (Hannan & Freeman, 1977). Boeker (1988) emphasizes the role of vested interests in creating organizational inertia, including capital investments, specialized skills and knowledge, and political processes.

Internal sources of inertia can be traced to an organization's need for reliability, accountability, coordination, and control. According to Hannan and Freeman (1984), accountability and reliability are necessary for organizations to achieve legitimacy and are thereby an integral part of success. The achievement of reliability and accountability means that organizational activities must be reproducible and therefore require the implementation of standardized routines and the institutionalization of activities. As a result, organizations tend to develop a resistance to change. In effect, the properties that make organizations accountable, reliable, and reproducible also make them inertial (Hannan & Freeman, 1984). Tushman and Romanelli view inertia in a similar manner:

> Internal requirements for coordinated action and flows, and external requirements for accountability and predictability are associated with increased social and structural complexity. Increased social and structural complexity engenders patterns of interdependence among activity systems, which promotes further convergence upon an established strategic orientation and resistance to fundamental change (1985: 191).

In short, organizational needs for legitimacy and reliability create complexity, institutionalization, and standardization. These properties, in turn, are associated with greater inertial characteristics and thereby reduce an organization's ability to adapt. Hannan and Freeman (1984) go so far as to say that inertial properties are actually required for survival, since firms which are not reliable and accountable will be selected out.

DiMaggio and Powell (1983) suggest a number of factors which increase the institutionalization of the organization and thereby increase its inertial tendencies (Romanelli, 1989). Coercive pressures are constraints on organizational actions which are "imposed by extra-organizational actors who come to understand that a particular way of doing business is appropriate and effective" (Romanelli, 1989: 227). Mimetic pressures arise from the uncertainty organizations face and result due to the tendency of organizations to imitate other organizations rather than approach practices in a rational, pragmatic manner. Normative pressures constrain organizational activities through educational standards and behavioral norms (Romanelli, 1989).

In summary, the population ecology perspective proposes that organizations are inertial in their ability to adapt to environmental variation. Inertia stems from the need for reliability and accountability as well as from coercive, mimetic, and normative pressures. Environmental change creates opportunities for the creation of new firms with forms that can utilize the resources available in the new environment.

Community Ecology

Community ecology represents a level of analysis which is one step above that of population ecology. In short, community ecology examines the interactions between numerous populations of organizational forms (Astley, 1985). As a result, community ecology can answer a number of questions which population ecology cannot (Astley, 1985). This perspective enables examination of how populations of organizations interact and how entire populations of organizations are created or cease to exist.

The community concept of open environmental space is of particular relevance to new venture formations. Astley (1985) argues that new organizational populations will emerge only when the environment is vacant and the new population will not be crowded out by other populations. Thus, open environmental space is a precursor to the creation of new organizations (Romanelli, 1989).

Empirical Evidence

Empirical research in the population ecology literature suggests that a relationship between institutional change and organizational foundings does exist. Delacroix and Carroll (1983) demonstrate a relation between political turmoil and the foundings of newspapers in Argentina and Ireland. The results show that national political turbulence is responsible for the increased establishment of newspapers. In another study of newspaper foundings, Carroll and Huo (1986) find that institutional environmental variables impact rates of founding and failure but do not affect the performance of these organizations. Both of these studies have been interpreted as meaning that institutional changes release resources that entrepreneurs can use to establish organizations (Wholey & Brittain, 1986). In a study of the founding rates of labor unions (Hannan & Freeman 1987), environmental conditions affected the founding of labor unions, but the environmental effects did not override ecological impacts (effects of density, and prior foundings and failures) on foundings. Tucker, Singh, Meinhard, and House (1988) also provide evidence of a relationship between institutional change and the founding of organizations (in this case, voluntary social services organizations). However, contrary to Hannan and Freeman's results, the Tucker et al. results show that institutional change does alter the nature of ecological processes. Tucker, Singh, and Meinhard (1990) find that both ecological processes and institutional change have greater impact on the founding of specialist organizations than generalist organizations. Overall, empirical research in the population ecology literature supports a relationship between longitudinal institutional change and the founding of organizations.

We have discussed the role of market disequilibrium, industry dynamics, and organizational inertia in encouraging entrepreneurship and new venture formation. Next, the discussion will move to industrial organization economics perspectives on the role of entry barriers in discouraging entry into industries. These perspectives have important implications for understanding new venture formations in industries.

ENTRY BARRIERS

Industrial organization economists have addressed the topic of entry barriers and the effect that they have on the profitability of and rate of entry into an industry. Entry, to the industrial organization economist, acts to discipline market incumbents and can upset the traditional structural characteristics of the industry (Geroski, Gilbert, & Jacquemin, 1990). In this regard, industrial organization economists are interested in characterizing industries relative to their amenability to entrants. The central tenet is that industries that are readily entered will charge competitive prices and not earn economic profits. Industries with structural or strategic characteristics resistant to new entrants will likely capture economic profits and therefore be socially inefficient. Entry barriers, then, are seen as an important determinant of the efficiency of markets.

In applying entry barrier theory to the understanding of *new venture formations*, researchers must be aware of the perspective taken by industrial organization economists. First, researchers must be careful to distinguish between the concept of entry as viewed by industrial organization economists and that of new venture formations. More specifically, entry is a broader concept that concerns the entry of organizations into an industry which previously did not serve that industry. From the economists' perspective, entry is inclusive of existing firms diversifying into an industry and new firms created to serve the relevant industry. Thus, the industrial organization economists' concept of entry is relevant to the study of new venture creation, but the ideas must be carefully applied so as not to misinterpret theoretical propositions or empirical results which are relevant to diversifying entrants but not to new venture formations (the dependent variable of the present research). The second difference in the industrial organization economists' perspective is a concern with the welfare economic implications of entry conditions in a market. A statement by Gersoki et al. exemplifies the dichotomy between the perspective of industrial organization economists and that taken herein.

> Although one may be interested in entry per se as an interesting phenomena to explain, the broader concern in looking at entry is, of course, with assessing market performance (1990: 3).

The present study does not represent an effort to assess market performance (social efficiency) as related to entry, but is concerned with the determinants of organizational foundings per se. Economic research concerned with the welfare implications of entry must be interpreted appropriately.

The discussion below presents a review of the relevant literature on the effect of entry barriers on new venture formations. Theoretical perspectives on entry barriers are reviewed in order to explicate the expected effect of entry barriers on new-firm entrepreneurship. Empirical evidence on the relationship between entry barriers and entry is extensive (relative to other empirical studies on determinants of new firm foundings) and is intermingled with the theoretical ideas presented below.

Bain (1956) was probably the first author to comprehensively address entry barriers and, as he termed it, "the condition of entry." He defines the condition of entry as

> ... the advantages of established sellers in an industry over potential entrant sellers, these advantages being reflected in the extent to which established sellers can persistently raise their prices above a competitive level without attracting new firms to enter the industry (Bain, 1956: 3).

Bain's definition focuses upon the difference between the profit an entrant would achieve post-entry and that which is enjoyed by incumbents prior to entry (Geroski et. al., 1990). An alternative definition of barriers to entry was put forth by Stigler (For a short

comparative discussion of various author's definitions of entry barriers
see Gilbert (1989: 476)):

> A barrier to entry may be defined as a cost of producing
> (at some or every level of output) which must be borne by
> a firm which seeks to enter an industry but is not borne by
> firms already in the industry (1968: 67)

As such, barriers to entry are often associated with a relative cost
advantage which accrues to incumbent firms (Caves, 1967; Bain, 1956).
The greater the relative disadvantage that non-incumbent firms face, the
greater the height of barriers to entry in a given industry. In short, due
to various factors that raise barriers to entry, incumbent firms possess
an asymmetrical advantage in serving a market that acts to exclude
entrants (Gilbert, 1989). In addition, empirical research has indicated
that the advantage incumbents hold is more important relative to new
firm entrants than it is to diversifying firms (Gorecki, 1975). In other
words, entry barriers tend to have more impact on new-firm entry. The
effect of barriers, therefore, may be especially important to the rates of
formation of new ventures.

Types of Entry Barriers

Entry barriers include a variety of factors which make entry by
non-incumbent firms difficult. Barriers to entry can be established by
pricing, plant location, and product differentiation/proliferation (Scherer,
1980). Economies of scale (Bain, 1956), and significant sunk costs
(Baumol, Panzar & Willig, 1982) have also been argued to deter entry.
Other possible entry barriers include government regulation, incumbent
retaliation, access to distribution, and proprietary knowledge such as
patents, copyrights, and trade secrets (Porter, 1985).

Bain (1956) considers three categories of barriers to entry:
1) an absolute cost advantage of incumbent firms over potential
entrants, 2) product differentiation advantages, and 3) economies of
scale. An absolute cost advantage exists when the production cost of
an entrant or potential entrant lies above that of incumbents (Caves,
1967). An absolute cost advantage can accrue from a variety of
conditions. First, a cost advantage may be associated with control of
superior production techniques (Bain, 1956) through patents, trade
secrets, etc. (Caves, 1967). Von Weizsacker refers to this type of
advantage as superior efficiency on the part of incumbents (1980).

Absolute cost advantages may also accrue from superior access to factors of production or a lower cost of capital (Bain, 1956). Product differentiation, economies of scale, and industry-concentration-related entry barriers are discussed below.

Product differentiation and advertising. Product differentiation advantages have been associated with established brand names, company reputations, control of superior product design, and control of favored distribution (Bain, 1956). In addition, buyer switching costs (buyer dis-utility from changing brands) may create product differentiation barriers (Gilbert, 1989). Bain (1956) argues that product differentiation is the strongest source of barriers to entry. Product differentiation results from differences in the actual qualities of products or from the reputation of a firm or brand name (Gilbert, 1989). Put differently, product differentiation occurs when buyers do not consider goods as being perfect substitutes. Porter (1985) describes differentiation as a generic strategy whereby the producers offer something unique that represents value added to buyers. As a result, the producer of one product brand cannot perfectly imitate another brand in the consumer's mind (Gilbert, 1989). The differentiated product may thereby represent a barrier to entry to new firms.

Advertising levels and, more generally, selling expenses, have often been considered as an indicator of product differentiation and thereby considered to be measures of entry barriers within industries. Bain (1956) argues that advertising is one of the factors that contributes most to product differentiation. To Williamson (1963), selling expenses allow firms to take advantage of any product differentiation advantages. The basic argument for selling expense as a barrier to entry is that it creates customer loyalty to products and thereby inhibits the entry of new producers (Scherer & Ross, 1990).

Advertising is indicative of product differentiation in two respects (Comanor & Wilson, 1967). First of all, high levels of advertising provide evidence that a product is actually differentiatable. Second, advertising levels are to some extent a determinant of the level of product differentiation. The second aspect might be especially true for situations where consumers have difficulty perceiving product attributes and therefore rely heavily on advertising for information relative to product offerings (Demsetz, 1982). In either case, Comanor and Wilson (1967) conclude that advertising is a useful measure of product differentiation.

Advertising is a barrier to entry in that it forces new entrants to sell at prices below established brands or to incur significant selling costs (Comanor & Wilson, 1967). Advertising as a component of product differentiation impacts entry barriers in three ways (Comanor & Wilson, 1967). First, advertising creates additional costs for entrants which occur at all levels of output. Higher levels of advertising relative to incumbents are required in order to induce consumer switching and to overcome buyer inertia and loyalty. Incumbent firms may already have built customer loyalty through prior advertising expenditures. Thus, older firms have been able to spread the cost of brand awareness over past sales and thereby possess an *a-priori* advantage over entrant firms which do not possess a corporate or brand history. A statement by Demsetz reflects this theory:

> New firms and recent entrants by virtue of their shorter histories or absence of specific investments may not be able to impart to consumers, without some compensating effort, the same confidence as has already been secured by older firms through past investments in good performance (1982: 50).

Since entrants have to induce customers to switch brands or overcome incumbent reputations, incumbents have an absolute cost advantage relative to new entrants.

Second, economies of scale exist in advertising (Comanor & Wilson, 1967; Spence, 1980). Since advertising is somewhat of a fixed cost (Spence, 1980), economies of scale exist due to the fact that messages can be spread over more volume at higher sales levels. Comanor and Wilson (1967: 425) termed this the "increasing effectiveness of advertising messages per unit of output." As such, an advantage to incumbents will occur if they can spread selling expenditures over a greater volume of sales (Scherer & Ross, 1990). Economies of scale are also created from "the decreasing costs for each advertising message purchased" (Comanor & Wilson, 1967: 426). Economies of scale in advertising result in barriers to entry due to the fact that small-scale entrants suffer a cost disadvantage.

Advertising also represents an entry barrier due to the additional capital required for entry into industries with high advertising levels (Comanor & Wilson, 1967). New entrants need to make a greater initial investment to effectively compete in an industry with high levels of advertising. In addition, the capital spent on advertising may represent a stronger barrier than some other capital expenditures, since advertising expenditures are sunk costs (Kessides, 1986). Since sunk costs are, by definition, unrecoverable in the case of failure, they are typically considered strong entry barriers (for a discussion of the role of sunk costs as barriers to entry see Baumol, et al., 1982).

As can be seen in Table II-2, empirical studies on the relation between entry and levels of industry advertising have mostly shown a negative association. However, some studies have found insignificance. The variability in the empirical evidence on this relationship is likely due to differences in entry measures, sample characteristics, and data sources. The authors had specific views of the meaning of entry and measured the concept accordingly. Again it is important to note that each of these researchers was approaching the subject of entry as an industrial organization economist and was concerned with the effect of entry on industry structure. In contrast, the present research is not directly concerned with structural effects, but attempts to explain rates of new venture formation. Thus, the results of these studies should be considered in context.

Of the studies below, the ones that measure entry most similarly to the present research are those of Shapiro and Khemani (1987) and MacDonald (1986). Both studies use a gross entry measure which by definition does not subtract exits from the number of entrants. Neither author calculates entry as a ratio of the number of enterprises in the industry. In addition, both studies exclude diversifying entrants from the measure of entry. The Shapiro and Khemani results support the existence of a relation between advertising and new business formations, while the MacDonald study finds no significant relation. The lack of findings in the MacDonald study may be attributable to a number of factors. Relative to Shapiro and Khemani, MacDonald analyzes a much more limited number of manufacturing industries (food and tobacco industries only). Also, Shapiro and Khemani may have specified the form of the relation in a superior manner. That is, by using the logarithm of entry, they suggest that the *rate* of entry is related to the advertising to sales ratio. Since MacDonald did not apply a logarithmic transformation, an empirical relation may not have been evident.

In summary, research has provided mixed results on the relation between entry and advertising levels. After sample, measurement, and specification issues are considered, few studies exist which are directly parallel to the questions on new venture formations in manufacturing industries. Those studies which are most closely related to questions of new venture formations are encouraging but nonetheless inconclusive. Additional research is needed in order to conclude that advertising serves as a barrier to the creation of new firms.

Economies of scale. Economies of scale have been argued to create barriers to entry in a number of ways. Scale economies can

TABLE II-2: EMPIRICAL STUDIES OF THE RELATION BETWEEN ADVERTISING AND ENTRY

Author	Measure of Entry	Results
Acs & Audretsch (1989)	Net small-firm entry as a percentage of the total number of firms	No relation
Shapiro & Khemani (1987)	Log of Gross Entry	Negative relation
Highfield & Smiley (1987)	Gross new incorporations as a percentage of the total number of corporations minus the average entry rate across all industries	No relation
MacDonald (1986)	Gross Entry of Establishments	No relation
Harrigan (1983a)	Dichotomous variable	Negative relation
Yip (1982)	Dichotomous variable	Negative relation in consumer-durables. No relation in other markets
Harrigan (1981)	Dichotomous variable	Positive relation
Harris (1976)	Entrant market share	Negative relation
Gorecki (1975)	1. Net entry of diversifying enterprises as a ratio to the total number of enterprises	No relation
	2. Net entry of specialist enterprises as a ratio to the total number of enterprises	Mixed Results
Orr (1974)	Log of net new incorporations	Negative relation

inhibit both large and small scale entry (Caves, 1967). Small scale entry occurs at an output less than the minimum efficient scale. The consideration of scale economies as a barrier to small-scale entry has led to the development of limit-price theory (Gilbert, 1989). Bain (1956) argues that economies of scale represent a barrier to large-scale entry through both a percentage effect and an absolute capital requirement effect. The percentage effect refers to the impact that entry of a minimum efficient scale plant (large-scale entry) has on total industry capacity. In situations where economies of scale exist, large-scale entry is inhibited by the negative price effect of the entrant's additional capacity. Capacity utilization levels therefore have an important barrier effect on large-scale entrants and may even impact small-scale entrants. Bain's absolute capital requirement effect results from the large capital investment needed to establish a plant in an industry with large economies of scale (Geroski et. al., 1990). In general, economies of scale as a barrier to entry will tend to be greater when the minimum efficient scale is a large portion of total industry output, and when unit costs rise rapidly just below the minimum efficient scale quantity (Bain, 1956).

In summary, economies of scale are an important consideration to potential entrants and their entry decision. Small-scale entry is often inhibited by the pricing practices of incumbents (a concern of limit-price theory). Large-scale entry is especially inhibited in industries which have low capacity utilization and capital requirements act to dissuade both large and small scale entry. The effect of limit pricing, capacity utilization, and capital requirements are discussed below.

Limit-price theory. Limit-price theory has been used to analyze the situation in which a dominant firm faces the threat of entry or expansion of small-scale competitors (Scherer & Ross, 1990). More specifically, limit-price theory considers the situation of a dominant firm (or group of firms acting as one) and fringe competitors (Gilbert, 1989). The limit price is defined as the price just below the level which will motivate fringe firms to enter the industry (fringe firms are said to assume that the dominant firm will continue to maintain its pre-entry level of output after entry) (Scherer & Ross, 1990). By setting its price at the limit price, the dominant firm can effectively discourage entry. The limit price lies above marginal cost due to the fact that fringe firms are producing at a quantity below minimum efficient scale (Scherer & Ross, 1990). In any case, the limit-price model provides theoretical justification for viewing economies of scale as a barrier to entry. Potential entrants which produce below minimum efficient scale are at a cost disadvantage and will be dissuaded from entry unless the dominant firm raises price above the limit price. Entry at larger scales can also be dissuaded by economy of scale-related entry barriers.

Large-scale entry and capacity utilization. Low levels of industry capacity utilization (high excess capacity) have been argued to act as a barrier to entry, especially to large-scale entrants. If economies of scale are large relative to total industry output, the entrance of a large-scale firm will often increase industry capacity such that industry prices will decline unless incumbents reduce output levels (Scherer & Ross, 1990). Scherer and Ross summarize this situation as follows:

The problem, in essence, is that a firm con-templating entry on a large scale has reason to fear that its incremental output will be absorbed by the market only if the price is reduced. As a result, even though the entrant's costs may be just as low as those of enterprises already in the industry, and even though the pre-entry price exceeds the entrant's full expected unit cost, the price after entry may fall below that cost, and entry will prove unprofitable. If this is anticipated, entry will be deterred (Scherer & Ross, 1990: 374).

In short, the effect that large-scale entry has on the market price in industries with significant economies of scale is likely to inhibit the entrance of large-scale firms. This effect will be more severe if existing capacity is high relative to demand. Low capacity utilization levels will already be putting price pressure on the incumbent firms, and the added capacity of a large-, or even small-scale entrant will likely reduce profitability levels. Potential entrants viewing such a situation will likely be dissuaded from entering.

Researchers have also argued that the addition of plant capacity (likely resulting in lower capacity utilization) can be used as a means of strategic entry deterrence (Wenders, 1971; Dixit, 1982; Spence, 1977). The central tenet of these authors is that investment in additional capacity makes valid the pre-entry threat of post-entry predatory pricing. The threat becomes valid due to the additional sunk costs that the excess capacity creates (Dixit, 1982). Potential entrants, knowing that the incumbent is committed to its current output level, will not choose to enter the industry (Dixit, 1982).

In sum, excess industry capacity (low-capacity utilization) can act as a barrier to entry. First, the greater the amount of excess capacity, the more likely that price will fall below cost, and the less likely that large-scale producers will enter the industry. Second, incumbent investments in excess capacity act as a signal of a willingness to fight price wars with entrants.

While the theoretical arguments linking capacity and entry have been strong, empirical research has been minimal. Those studies that have been performed seem to have shown a negative relation between excess capacity and entry. Harrigan (1983a) reports that excess capacity acts as a barrier to entry. Hilke (1984) finds that the existence of excess capacity tends to dissuade entrants, but his results are not significant. In contrast, Lieberman (1987) finds that incumbents rarely utilize excess capacity as a barrier to entry. Again, these studies should be interpreted with care, since the entry measures were not directly parallel to the concept of new-firm formations.

Capital requirements have also been suggested as a barrier to entry, which is related to economies of scale in an industry. The paragraphs below discuss capital requirements as a barrier to entry.

Economies of scale serve as a barrier to entry in another manner which Bain refers to as the "absolute-capital-requirement effect" (1956: 55). Where the minimum efficient scale is significant, the capital needed to enter an industry may be such that few potential entrants will be able to secure the required funding without being placed at a cost disadvantage due to higher capital costs. In contrast, contestable market theory implies that economies of scale and capital requirements do not represent a barrier to entry unless the initial capital requirement represents a sunk cost (Baumol, et. al., 1982). Markets which do not require an unrecoverable investment are argued to be completely contestable since entrants can easily dispose of investments if failure would occur. The airline industry typically serves as an example of a contestable market since the market for airplanes is relatively efficient. In short, the theory of contestable markets implies that capital requirements do not necessarily represent barriers to entry. However, markets which do require investment in sunk costs will still contain entry barriers which result from capital requirements. In some markets, much of the investment made in capital could be considered to be sunk (Schmalensee, 1988). Dixit (1982) argues that in most instances, production activity requires sunk costs. Thus, in many industries (especially, perhaps, manufacturing industries) it is reasonable to assume that large initial capital requirements are sunk and therefore represent barriers to entry. Also, Baumol (1982) admits that the conditions leading to perfectly contestable markets are more of an ideal than a reality.

The argument for capital requirements as a barrier to entry has also been criticized since it relies somewhat on the assumption of imperfect capital markets (Schmalensee, 1988). According to this argument, a perfect capital market would not discriminate between an entrant and an incumbent relative to the distribution of capital and conditions thereof. This criticism is only partially valid, especially for new-firm entrants. First of all, the differential capital raising ability of incumbents relative to entrants may be due to asymmetric information regarding a potential entrant's opportunity and capability (Schmalensee, 1988). In other words, capital providers are likely to have more information regarding an incumbent's potential versus a new entrant's investment potential. Second, the history and prior activities of incumbent firms are likely to signal lenders regarding the risk level of a capital commitment.

> But there is no reason to believe that such a history is irrelevant to the interest payments required by lenders. Larger, older firms generally will be able to borrow more cheaply than smaller, younger firms (Demsetz 1982: 50).

Demsetz's statement emphasizes the role which firm history and legitimacy play in their ability to gain favorable treatment when acquiring capital. Thus, it is reasonable to assume that new-firm entrants will often encounter absolute cost disadvantages resulting from higher capital costs related to capital requirements.

Various authors have investigated the empirical relationship between capital requirements and entry (See Table II-3). Most researchers have shown a negative relation between capital requirements and entry, and indicate that capital requirements represent a pervasive barrier to entry (Shapiro & Khemani, 1987; MacDonald, 1986; Hamilton, 1985; Orr, 1974; Mansfield, 1962). However, some authors did not find a significant negative relationship (Acs & Audretsch, 1989; Highfield & Smiley, 1987; Harrigan, 1983a; Harris, 1976). Again, there is some concern resulting from the variability in samples, data sources, measures of capital requirements, and perhaps most importantly, measures of entry. As discussed above, the two studies which are most similar to the questions and agenda of the present study are those of MacDonald (1986) and Shapiro and Khemani (1987). Both of these studies find a negative relation between capital requirements and unadjusted gross entry. The results of Hamilton (1985) are also interesting relative to the present research, and may explain why some of the other studies did not find a significant effect of capital requirements. Hamilton tested the impact of capital requirements on dependent versus independent businesses and found that capital requirements act as barriers to entry only for independent businesses. Since the present study is concerned with new venture formations, Hamilton's results are particularly relevant. In addition, they also may indicate that the reason other authors did not find a negative relationship was due to the grouping of independent and dependent firms in their measures of entry. Theoretically, Hamilton's results may support the contention that capital is more difficult or costly to acquire for new firms than existing firms. Overall, the empirical evidence on capital requirements and entry suggests that capital requirements will likely serve as a barrier to the formation of new firms.

TABLE II-3: EMPIRICAL STUDIES
OF THE RELATION BETWEEN CAPITAL
REQUIREMENTS AND ENTRY

Author	Measure of Entry	Results
Acs & Audretsch (1989)	Net small-firm entry as a percentage of the total number of firms	No relation
Shapiro & Khemani (1987)	Log of Gross Entry	Negative relation
Highfield & Smiley (1987)	Gross new incorporations as a percentage of the total number of corporations minus the average entry rate across all industries	No relation
MacDonald (1986)	Gross Entry of Establishments	Negative relation
Hamilton (1985)	1. Gross new independent businesses divided by the total number of businesses	Negative relation
	2. Gross new dependent businesses divided by the total number of businesses	No relation
Harrigan (1983a)	Dichotomous variable	No relation
Harris (1976)	Entrant market share	Positive relation
Orr (1974)	Log of net new incorporations	Negative relation
Mansfield (1962)	Net firm entry as proportion of total number of firms	Negative relation

Industry concentration. The relation between industry concentration and entry has been discussed by a number of authors. Theoretical arguments can be made for both a positive and negative relation between these two variables (Highfield & Smiley, 1987). The more traditional approach is that high concentration results in the ability of incumbent firms to collude in order to thwart the activities of new entrants (Orr, 1974). In contrast, small-scale entry into a concentrated industry may go unnoticed, since the entrant does not have a significant impact on total industry output (Duetsch, 1975). As a result, the small-scale entrant may be able to share the benefits of a collusive, concentrated industry environment (Duetsch, 1975). Since concentrated industries generally exhibit higher profit rates (Harrigan, 1981), there may be a greater attraction to enter. In addition, lower concentration may deter entry to the extent that large scale entry may force the entrant to operate below minimum efficient scale (Baron, 1973; Highfield & Smiley, 1987).

Since the theoretical arguments on industry concentration and entry have been dichotomous in their prediction, empirical studies may be the key to determining the direction of the effect (Duetsch, 1975). "Whether in fact the net rate of entry is greater in concentrated or unconcentrated industries can only be determined, it appears, by turning to the evidence" (Duetsch, 1975: 452).

A number of empirical studies have shown a negative relation between industry concentration and entry (Acs & Audretsch 1989; Shapiro & Khemani, 1987; Harrigan, 1981; Orr, 1974).   (See Table II-4.) In contrast, other authors have found that either no relation exists (Yip, 1982; Highfield & Smiley, 1987) or that the relation is actually positive (Harris, 1976; Duetsch, 1975). The mixed results on the impact of concentration do not shed any additional light on the theoretical arguments discussed above.   Again, variability in the empirical methodologies (measures, samples, and model specifications) may be responsible for varied results. Also, it is important to consider which studies are most applicable to the study of new venture formations as opposed to the study of industry entry. As discussed before, the Shapiro and Khemani (1987) study uses a measure of entry that is closest to the concept of new venture formations. These authors report a negative effect of concentration on the logarithm of gross entry in manufacturing industries. Hamilton (1985) evidences a positive effect of concentration on dependent businesses, and a negative effect on independent businesses. Acs and Audretsch (1989) also shows a negative relation in a study which examines the entry of small firms. Taken together, these three studies suggest that a negative relation might be expected between industry concentration and the creation of new firms.

The Attractiveness of Entry

Entry inducements. For some time, industrial organization economics researchers have recognized that factors other than entry barriers impact the rate of entry into industries. Bhagwati (1970: 305) discusses the theoretical importance of existing firm price premiums to the "attractiveness of entry." Gorecki (1975: 140) suggests that certain "entry-inducing" factors are important determinants of entry. Such entry inducements have been argued to be a function of the profitability

TABLE II-4: EMPIRICAL STUDIES
OF THE RELATION BETWEEN INDUSTRY
CONCENTRATION AND ENTRY

Author	Measure of Entry	Results
Acs & Audretsch (1989)	Net small-firm entry as a percentage of the total number of firms	Negative relation
Shapiro & Khemani (1987)	Log of Gross Entry	Negative relation
Highfield & Smiley (1987)	Gross new incorporations as a percentage of the total number of corporations minus the average entry rate across all industries	No relation
Hamilton (1985)	1. Gross new independent businesses divided by the total number of businesses	Negative relation
	2. Gross new dependent businesses divided by the total number of businesses	Positive relation
Yip (1982)	Dichotomous variable	No relation
Harrigan (1981)	Dichotomous variable	Negative relation
Harris (1976)	Entrant market share	Positive relation
Duetsch (1975)	Percentage change in number of independent firms (net entry) in the industry	Positive relation
Orr (1974)	Log of net new incorporations	Negative relation

which entrants expect after entry, and potential industry profitability is related to 1) past industry profitability, 2) industry growth rate, and 3) technical progress (Highfield & Smiley, 1987).

Numerous authors have viewed pre-entry profitability and growth rate as variables that encourage potential entrants. In addition, most empirical research on entry includes both of these entry inducements as predictors of entry. As shown in Table II-5, empirical research has been nearly unanimous in its support for a relation between industry growth and entry. Empirical research on the relationship between industry profitability and entry has been nearly as consistent in its findings (See Table II-6).

TABLE II-5: EMPIRICAL STUDIES
OF THE RELATION BETWEEN
INDUSTRY GROWTH AND ENTRY

Author	Measure of Entry	Results
Acs & Audretsch (1989)	Net small-firm entry as a percentage of the total number of firms	Positive relation
Shapiro & Khemani (1987)	Log of Gross Entry	Positive relation
Highfield & Smiley (1987)	Gross new incorporations as a percentage of the total number of corporations minus the average entry rate across all industries	Positive relation
MacDonald (1986)	Gross Entry of Establishments	Positive relation
Hamilton (1985)	1. Gross new independent businesses divided by the total number of businesses 2. Gross new dependent businesses divided by the total number of businesses	Positive relation
Hause & DuReitz (1984)	1. Employment share of new entrants 2. Number of firm entrants divided by total number of firms	Positive convex relation Positive convex relation
Yip (1982)	Dichotomous variable	Positive relation
Harrigan (1981)	Dichotomous variable	Positive relation
Harris (1976)	Entrant market share	No relation
Gorecki (1975)	1. Net entry of diversifying enterprises as a ratio to the total number of enterprises 2. Net entry of specialist enterprises as a ratio to the total number of enterprises	Positive relation Positive relation
Duetsch (1975)	Percentage change in number of independent firms (net entry) in the industry	Positive relation
Orr (1974)	Log of net new incorporations	Weak positive relation

TABLE II-6: EMPIRICAL STUDIES
OF THE RELATION BETWEEN INDUSTRY
PROFITABILITY AND ENTRY

Author	Measure of Entry	Results
Acs & Audretsch (1989)	Net small-firm entry as a percentage of the total number of firms	Positive relation
Shapiro & Khemani (1987)	Log of Gross Entry	Positive relation
Highfield & Smiley (1987)	Gross new incorporations as a percentage of the total number of corporations minus the average entry rate across all industries	Positive relation
MacDonald (1986)	Gross Entry of Establishments	No relation
Hamilton (1985)	1. Gross new independent businesses divided by the total number of businesses	No relation
	2. Gross new dependent businesses divided by the total number of businesses	Weak positive relation
Yip (1982)	Dichotomous variable	Positive relation
Harris (1976)	Entrant market share	Positive relation
Duetsch (1975)	Percentage change in number of independent firms (net entry) in the industry	No relation
Orr (1974)	Log of net new incorporations	Weak positive relation
Mansfield (1962)	Net firm entry as proportion of total number of firms	Positive relation

Highfield and Smiley propose that "a high rate of technical progress in an industry will also indicate a dynamic and evolving situation and thus might attract new entrants seeking to discover and develop new products and processes" (1987: 58). Acs and Audretsch suggest that "technological opportunity" (1989: 257) may also encourage entry, but add that technologically intense industries possess scale disadvantages in research and development that act as barriers to entry, especially to small firms. Thus, the technological intensity of an industry may impact entry in two ways: 1) technical progress creates opportunities whereby potential entrants may gain an advantage through innovative activity, 2) technological intensity creates a scale disadvantage which deters entry. Although not completely consistent, the empirical results shown in Table II-7 support a stronger barrier effect of technological intensity.

Entry Gateways

Yip (1982) expands on traditional approaches to entry and entry barriers by suggesting that the number of additional factors impact rates of entry. In short, Yip took a corporate strategy perspective on entry barriers and argues that the skills and assets of potential entrants, and the availability of "unique competitive strategies" (1982: 129) can create gateways to entry which allow entrants to overcome or avoid barriers. Yip proposes four classifications of variables which impactrates of entry into industries. These include the traditional barriers and inducements to entry as well as disequilibrium effects and heterogeneity effects. Disequilibrium effects refer to short-run factors which contribute to excess demand and therefore ease entry into an industry. (A more extensive discussion of Yip's thoughts on industry disequilibrium is presented at the beginning of this chapter). Heterogeneity effects represent the potential of a firm to approach an industry in a variety of unique configurations based on differences in product features, promotion, distribution, and others. Pursuing industries through a heterogeneous strategy may allow entrants to avert differentiation barriers or avoid cost or scale barriers. Empirical variables which Yip uses as measures of industry heterogeneity include investment intensity, advertising intensity, research and development intensity, and selling intensity. Yip's discussions on heterogeneity are similar to the ideas of Porter (1981). Porter suggests that the difficulty of entry into an industry is dependent on the strategy which the potential entrant adopts. Or, in other words, the difficulty of entry is dependent upon the strategic group to which the entrant wishes to belong. It is easier for entrants to enter some strategic groups than others, and strategic group membership determines the level of profitability the entrant will achieve.

Another contribution of Yip's study is his recognition that many of the variables typically used in empirical studies of entry can have an effect relative to more than one of the four classes of entry determining variables. For example, advertising intensity is argued to have both a barrier and heterogeneity effect relative to entry. The

TABLE II-7: EMPIRICAL STUDIES
OF THE RELATION BETWEEN
TECHNOLOGICAL INTENSITY AND ENTRY

Author	Measure of Entry	Results
Acs & Audretsch (1989)	Net small-firm entry as a percentage of the total number of firms	Negative relation to R&D intensity Positive relation to small-firm innovation rate
Shapiro & Khemani (1987)	Log of Gross Entry	No relation to the % of scientists and engineers
Highfield & Smiley (1987)	Gross new incorporations as a percentage of the total number of corporations minus the average entry rate across all industries	Positive relation to R&D intensity
Yip (1982)	Dichotomous variable	No relation to R&D intensity
Orr (1974)	Log of net new incorporations	Negative relation to R&D intensity

multiple effect of many of the empirical measures may account for many of the non-findings in prior empirical studies of entry, as well as for the inconsistency in results across studies.

Recently, Kunkel and Hofer suggested that the overall "ease of entry" (1991: 6) into an industry is a function of entry barriers and entry gateways, and that entry gateways can be classified as structural or resource gateways. Structural entry gateways include factors such as market segmentation, diversity of competitors, gross margins, and incumbent commitments to technologies. Resource entry gateways include access to distribution, access to supplies, access to technologies, and others.

Summary

In summary, care must be taken in applying the industrial organization economics literature on entry barriers to the study of venture formations. First of all, the economists' definition of entry varies from the more narrow concept of new venture formations. Second, much of the purpose of entry barrier research is to understand the industry performance implications of the condition of entry. Nonetheless, theoretical and empirical evidence supports the existence of a relation between entry barriers and entry, and these findings can be usefully applied to the understanding of the determinants of new venture formations. A number of entry barriers can reasonably be expected to be related to firm foundings. These include, but are not limited to, product differentiation, economies of scale, and industry concentration. In addition, discussions of entry inducements and entry gateways are important to understanding the factors which may attract new ventures to an industry and allow them to avoid or overcome barriers to entry.

CHAPTER SUMMARY

This chapter reviews a number of streams of literature which are relevant to the understanding of the demand determinants of new venture creations. States of industry disequilibrium have been argued to create market opportunities which attract entrepreneurs and encourage the formation of new businesses. Industry dynamics are viewed as a primary cause of disequilibrium and are therefore important to understanding new business creations. Discussions by economists and organization theorists provide an understanding of the nature of industry change and its role in creating disequilibrium. These discussions also point to the role of organizational inertia in preventing incumbent firms from moving to opportunities and thereby encouraging new firm formations. Organization theorists, sociologists, economists, and population ecologists have all discussed organizational inertia, and a number of these perspectives have direct implications for explaining new venture creations. Finally, industrial organization economists' discussions of entry barriers are especially relevant to the understanding of new venture formations.

III

THEORETICAL DEVELOPMENT

Chapter Overview

Prior theoretical and empirical research in Austrian economics, industrial organization economics, and organization theory implies a model of demand determinants of new venture formations. This chapter presents a model of new venture creation based upon the concepts of industry dynamics, organizational inertia, and entry barriers. Figure III-1 provides a graphical representation of this model of new venture creation.

The view of entrepreneurship and new venture formations espoused herein is based upon an economic model of *dynamic* markets under the conditions of *imperfect* information and *heterogeneous* demand. The theoretical framework is based extensively on the work of a number of authors addressing the topics of disequilibrium and entrepreneurship. Specifically, the theory relies heavily on the writings of Kirzner (1973, 1979, 1983), Mises (1949), Leibenstein (1968, 1979), Rizzo (1979), Knight (1921), Schultz (1975), Penrose (1959), and Rosen (1983). A detailed summary of each of these author's works is provided in the previous chapter. Conceptualizations of entry barriers and their impact on new venture formations are integrated into the framework. In addition, the role of organizational inertia in constraining existing firm activities is described.

This chapter is divided into two *major* sections. The first section develops the theoretical foundation of the model and presents a number of general *propositions*. Based on the propositions presented in the first section, the second section generates specific and empirically testable *hypotheses*.

The first major section is arranged in the following order. First, discussions of disequilibrium and market opportunity are

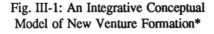

Fig. III-1: An Integrative Conceptual
Model of New Venture Formation*

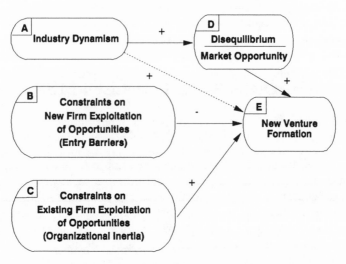

* (+) represents a positive relationship, and (-) a negative
relationship between variable dyads

presented. Then the relationship between industry dynamics and disequilibrium is examined and the types of change in industries are presented. Next the notion of alternative exploitation of market opportunities is introduced and constraints on existing firms and new ventures are discussed. This includes discussions of the role of entry barriers and organizational inertia in determining the rate of new venture formations. The proposed theoretical model is then analyzed relative to other discussions on industry dynamics and entrepreneurship.

As mentioned above, the second major section translates the propositions into testable hypotheses. Four hypotheses are developed relative to the relationship between industry change and new venture formation. Then, a number of hypotheses on entry barriers and organizational inertia and new venture formation are developed, bringing the total number of hypotheses to eleven.

The chapter concludes with a summary of the proposed model of new venture creation.

THEORETICAL DEVELOPMENT AND
PROPOSITIONS

Disequilibrium and Market Opportunity

A state of equilibrium exists when the different plans of individuals are mutually compatible (Hayek, 1948). In addition, "An equilibrium situation is one that exhibits no tendency to change and that can be derived logically from a model that incorporates the operation of opposing forces" (Rizzo, 1979: 4). Another characteristic of equilibrium, which might be seen as subsequent to the mutual compatibility condition, is that price is equal to marginal cost, and economic profits are absent (Scherer & Ross, 1990). In contrast, a state of disequilibrium is evidenced by the presence of opportunities for economic profit (Kirzner, 1973). Producers, for example, could produce a given product at a lower cost, sell at the present market price, and earn economic profits. Thus, the existence of market opportunities implies a state of market disequilibrium (Kirzner, 1973; Mises, 1949; Rizzo, 1979; Schultz, 1975). In short, disequilibrium is characterized by the presence of market opportunities. Market opportunities are productive possibilities which, when acted upon, can yield profits for economic actors.

Industry Dynamism, Disequilibrium, and Market Opportunity

What then are the factors that might lead to conditions of disequilibrium or, equivalently, market opportunity? The primary determinant of disequilibrium and, consequently, market opportunity, is change within an industry (Kirzner, 1973; Mises, 1949; Knight, 1921; Rosen, 1983). Authors of the Austrian tradition, such as Kirzner (1973) and Mises (1949) see change as fundamental to the creation of economic incentives in the market. To Mises, change in the the market results in a deviation from normal market conditions, and the subsequent creation of profit opportunities, or equivalently, disequilibrium. Change, by its very nature alters the underlying assumptions upon which production decisions are made. Thus, productive activities based on prior assumptions of market conditions are either inefficient, or no longer perfectly in concert with market needs, thereby creating a state of disequilibrium. For present purposes, industry change or, equivalently, industry dynamism, will refer to a variety of factors which alter the nature of demand or affect production possibilities.

Knight (1921) also recognizes the link between industry dynamism and opportunity, but is explicit in stating that the uncertainty of change is crucial to the creation of opportunity. To Knight, industry change is a necessary, but not sufficient condition for the creation of market opportunities. Predictable change does not create profit potential. Rather, uncertain change is necessary for opportunities to arise. Knight argues that if change could be predicted, producers could plan ahead and thereby efficiently eliminate any profit potential. "Dynamic changes give rise to a peculiar form of income only in so far as the changes and their consequences are unpredictable in character" (Knight, 1921: 37).

Kirzner (1973) essentially recognizes the role of uncertainty by arguing that entrepreneurs earn profit through superior alertness to opportunities. In fact, Kirzner's theoretical arguments depend upon asymmetrical alertness of entrepreneurs to opportunities created by industry dynamism. Given asymmetrical awareness to changes (or asymmetrical ability to react), it is possible for some market participants to earn economic profits. Mises (1949) views the success of market participants as depending on their ability to predict uncertainty regarding future conditions. Although presented differently, Rizzo (1979) also recognizes the importance of the uncertainty of change. To Rizzo, the most important variable is time. Uncertainty and surprise result from events that occur through the passage of time, and disequilibrium and the potential for profit thereby arise.

Essentially, these authors rely on the assumption of incomplete information on productive opportunities to validate the relations between change and market opportunity. Under conditions of perfect information, producers could equally predict industry events, plan accordingly, and thereby immediately eliminate any profit potential and instantaneously move the market to equilibrium. Thus, the greater the uncertain change within an industry, the greater the probability that market opportunity exists within that industry. Theoretically, uncertain change, rather than change itself, is the precursor to market opportunity and disequilibrium.

Despite theoretical support for the uncertain change/market opportunity link, it is empirically pragmatic to consider a linkage between change per se and market opportunity. First of all, it would be difficult (if not definitionally impossible) to empirically differentiate between uncertain change and predictable dynamics. The difficulty of distinguishing between these two types of change is supported by research which has shown that decision makers vary in their ability to scan the uncertain environment and use their predictive skills (Hambrick, 1982). Second, evidence does exist to imply that change, per se, can be viewed as uncertain. Duncan (1972) provides empirical support for the belief that environmental dynamism (the degree to which decision factors change over time) is related to uncertainty. Therefore, it may not be conceptually inconsistent to consider change per se to create market opportunity. It is expected that industry dynamics are highly related to the uncertainty facing firms in an industry.

In short, pragmatic considerations in measuring uncertain change necessitate the use of a coarser-grained approach than would be ideal. Proposing a relationship between change per se and market opportunity represents a good beginning until better operationalizations of uncertain change can be arrived at. The empirical analysis presented in the following chapters does not attempt to distinguish between uncertain and predictable industry change.

The above discussion leads to the development of Proposition 1, which can be summarized as follows: Changes in a market create a state of market disequilibrium whereby the needs of consumers are not perfectly matched to the offerings of producers. Disequilibrium, somewhat by definition, is characterized by the existence of market opportunities. Generally, the greater the industry dynamism, and the greater the unpredictability of that change, the greater will be the extent of disequilibrium created, and the more market opportunities that are created.

> *Proposition 1:* The greater the industry dynamism, the greater the market opportunity which exists within an industry.

Proposition 1 is illustrated as path A-D in Figure III-1. Given the importance of dynamism in creating market opportunities, a further explanation of the nature of such change is in order.

Types of Market Change

The classical viewpoints. Various economists have presented factors which account for the dynamism that occurs in industries. The discussions of these authors are extensively reviewed in Chapter II but will be summarized below for the reader's convenience. It is possible to synthesize the change factors discussed by these authors into five basic types of market dynamics.

Schumpeter describes five classes of "new combinations" (1934: 66) which represent areas in which change can occur in an industry. These include new products, new methods of production, new sources of supply, new markets, and new industry organizations. Kirzner (1973) presents a shorter list, which includes changes in human tastes, resource availability, and technological knowledge. Knight (1921) describes five types of generic change: population is increasing, capital is increasing, methods of production are improving, forms of industrial establishments are changing, and the wants of consumers are multiplying. Penrose (1963) has a list similar to Knight's, but refers to her list as the forces stimulating the growth of an economy. Included are population growth, technological advance leading to the development of new resources and of new industries, shifts in consumers' tastes, expansion of consumer wants, and increased savings and capital accumulation. Yip (1982) presents four factors which are argued to contribute to industry disequilibrium. These factors include the exit of competitors, technological change, new-product activity, and capacity utilization. Finally, Rosen (1983) discusses the non-routine changes of the creation of new markets, new goods, new services, and new ways of doing things.

A synthesis. The literature on change dynamics might be synthesized to five types of market change: 1) increases in demand, 2) modification of demand characteristics, 3) technological development, 4) new sources of supply, and 5) political/regulatory change. The first, and perhaps most obvious, source of industry dynamism is the expansion of demand. In this case, the total demand for a given industry's product increases without any modification of the nature of that demand. This can be characterized in traditional economic terms as a shift in the demand curve to the right: for any given price, the quantity demanded is greater.

The second type of industry dynamism is a modification of demand characteristics. This is often said to be a function of a change in human tastes and preferences. It can take any of several possible forms. Changes in tastes and preferences can cause an entirely new niche to arise, split a given industry demand into two or more niches, reduce one niche while increasing another, etc. The central idea is that changes in tastes and preferences modify the nature of the demand and thereby alter the type and quantity of products desired by consumers.

A third type of industry dynamism is technological development. Technological advance is, in one manner or the other, included in all of the aforementioned authors' lists. Technological development can be classified into product and process innovation. Product innovations can create entirely new niches, or even new industries. Such technological development can result in the possibility of minor product modifications, or can make entirely new products possible. Process innovations generally allow the possibility of more efficient methods of production, thereby introducing the possibility of lowering costs. However, such developments can also make an entirely new product possible.

A fourth type of industry dynamism is the availability of new sources of supply. New sources of supply usually make it possible for alert entrepreneurs to reduce the cost of producing a given product.

A fifth type of industry dynamism is political/regulatory. The classical authors discussed above do not include political and regulatory change as a major source of industry dynamism. However, in certain situations, the impact of governmental policies is significant (see, for example, Delacroix & Carroll, 1983; Bedeian & Zammuto, 1991). Political/regulatory change can be as mundane as a minor tax break for given methods of production, or can be as severe as the deregulation of an industry, such as has occurred in the telecommunications, airline, and banking industries.

Some of the types of industry dynamism discussed previously will be used in a later section to formulate specific hypotheses regarding industry dynamism and new venture formation. First, however, a discussion of entrepreneurship and new venture formation is in order.

Industry Dynamism, Market Opportunity, and Entrepreneurship

An interesting conceptualization of entrepreneurship emerges from the industry dynamism/market opportunity perspective. This conceptualization may provide fertile ground for understanding the entrepreneurial function. Entrepreneurship involves taking advantage of market opportunities through the direction of productive activities. Entrepreneurs are viewed as recognizing and acting upon opportunities and thereby moving the market towards equilibrium (Kirzner, 1973; Mises, 1949). In this conceptualization, entrepreneurship can be a function of existing organizations, or alternatively, associated with the creation of new organizations.

Entrepreneurial activity can therefore be predicted based upon the existence of market opportunities.

Proposition 2: The more market opportunities that exist in an industry (thus, the greater the disequilibrium), the greater the *entrepreneurial activity* within an industry.

Propositions 1 and 2 sketch a spectrum of cause and effect relationships shown in Figure III-2. These relationship can be summarized as follows: Industry changes create market opportunities (and a state of disequilibrium) which in turn increase the entrepreneurial activity within an industry. However, one might argue that industry change directly impacts entrepreneurial activity. This direct link is shown in Figure III-2 and is codified in Proposition 3.

Proposition 3: The greater the industry dynamism, the greater the rate of entrepreneurship within an industry.

Fig. III-2: Illustration of Propositions
1, 2, and 3

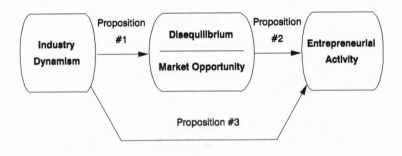

Proposition 3 is especially important since market opportunity, as conceptualized herein, is at least partially immeasurable. Market opportunity exists due to the uncertainty surrounding it. If market opportunity were known (and therefore measurable), the market would react accordingly and eliminate its existence. This is exemplified in the following statement by Kirzner:

> I would submit that the entrepreneurial function must necessarily always be that of sniffing out opportunities that on the surface do not appear to exist. Once a profit opportunity has become obvious, it no longer retains its character of a pure profit opportunity (1979: 149).

According to Kirzner, it would be impossible to measure the existence of profit opportunities, since the widespread knowledge of their existence would negate their existence. Sandberg (1986) takes a similar approach and does not attempt to measure disequilibrium itself, but examines factors from which disequilibrium is said to arise.

Some researchers have attempted to empirically analyze the concept of market opportunity by using price-cost margins and other industry profitability measures (Acs & Audretsch, 1989; Shapiro & Khemani, 1987). For the present conceptualization, however, this is viewed as inappropriate. While industry profitability measures may capture the existence of some opportunity in an industry, they cannot capture the really important opportunities that exist but are not evident to market participants. In sum, Proposition 3 posits a direct relationship between industry change and market opportunity. This proposition follows from Propositions 1 and 2 and is an empirical necessity.

Industry Dynamism, Market Opportunity, and New Venture Formation

The interest of the present research is to develop a conceptualization of new venture formation. However, to this point in the theoretical development, little has been said of new venture formation. Propositions 2 and 3 address the more general concept of entrepreneurship, of which new venture formation is a part. It may or may not be appropriate to assume that increased entrepreneurial activity will lead to increased new venture formation. In addition, a number of factors may impact whether this assumption is correct. These issues will be addressed shortly, but for now it is useful to assume that, other things equal, greater entrepreneurial activity will lead to greater new venture formations. Proposition 4 below modifies Proposition 3 to specifically address new venture formations.

Proposition 4:   Ceteris paribus, industry dynamism will be positively related to the rate of *new venture creation* within an industry.

The relationship between Propositions 3 and 4 and industry dynamism, entrepreneurial activity, and new venture formation are shown in Figure III-3.

The following paragraphs explore the assumption that increased entrepreneurial activity implies increased new venture formation. More specifically, they specify the factors which determine the extent to which new ventures, as opposed to existing firms, seize market opportunities.

Given a market which contains opportunity for economic profit, three outcomes are possible. The first and most disappointing to the prospect of economic development is that no firms take advantage of the opportunity and potential rents remain unexploited. According to

Fig. III-3: Illustration of Propositions
3 and 4

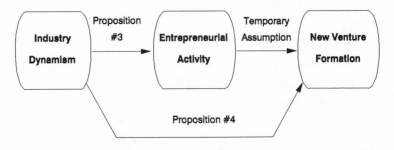

Penrose (1963), this might occur when firms do not see opportunities for expansion or are unwilling or unable to respond to them.   The second alternative outcome is that existing firms move to take advantage of the market opportunity. The third possibility, which is the focus of the present model, is that new ventures are created to exploit the opportunity.   Figure III-4 provides a visual representation of the possible outcomes subsequent to the creation of market opportunities.

The extent to which opportunities will be exploited, and the type of economic actor which exploits those opportunities will be a function of the constraints on existing firms, and the constraints on new

Fig. III-4: Alternative Exploitations of
Market Opportunities

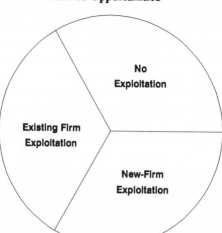

firms. These relations are illustrated in Figure III-1. The relative strengths of each of the constraints will determine what type of economic actor, if any, will take advantage of emerging opportunities. The greater the constraints on existing firms, the greater the rate of new business formations. On the other hand, the greater the constraints on new venture creation, the lesser the formation of new businesses. Two types of constraints are discussed below: entry barriers and organizational inertia. Entry barriers prevent new ventures from taking advantage of available opportunities, while organizational inertia precludes existing firms from exploiting opportunities. Generally speaking, higher entry barriers will increase the opportunities exploited by existing firms, and decrease those available to new firms. On the other hand, greater organizational inertia will decrease the percentage of existing firm exploitation and increase that of new firms.

Figure III-5 provides a decision-tree representation of the relation between constraints and alternative exploitation of existing opportunities. The reader needs to keep in mind that Figure III-5 is presented for illustrative purposes only and addresses situations where industry change has occurred and market opportunities exist. In industries where no organizational inertia exists and entry barriers are high, existing firms will likely exploit the opportunities created by market changes. Where neither inertia nor entry barriers exist, existing firm exploitation is likely, but new firms may also successfully exploit

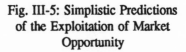

Fig. III-5: Simplistic Predictions
of the Exploitation of Market
Opportunity

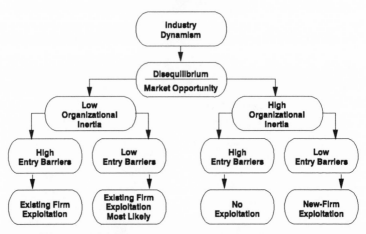

opportunities. In industries in which the existing firms are inertial and entry barriers are high, opportunities will be left unexploited. Where organizational inertia is high, and no entry barriers exist, new firms will be created to exploit available opportunities.

In summary, market dynamism creates a state of disequilibrium in which opportunities for profit are available for exploitation. The type of economic actor which exploits the available opportunities is dependent upon the constraints on existing firms, and the constraints on new venture formation. Organizational inertia constrains existing firms from moving toward opportunities, while entry barriers constrain the formation of new ventures in an industry. In the paragraphs below, entry barriers and organizational inertia are more thoroughly analyzed relative to their effects on new venture formations.

Constraints on Exploitation by New Ventures: Entry Barriers

Despite the existence of market opportunities within an industry, potential entrants can be dissuaded by the existence of entry barriers. "The ability of small firms to seize on profitable opportunities in which they can grow will be destroyed if barriers are erected against their entry . . . ." (Penrose, 1963: 228). Thus, opportunities, which might otherwise be open to new-entrant entrepreneurs, are unavailable due to factors which leave new firms at a disadvantage relative to incumbent firms. In short, due to various factors that raise barriers to entry, incumbent firms possess an asymmetrical advantage in serving a market that acts to exclude entrants (Gilbert, 1989). The lack of barriers to entry will allow entrepreneurs to establish new ventures to take advantage of market opportunities and thereby earn profits. In addition, empirical research has indicated that the advantage incumbents hold is more important relative to new-firm entrants than it is to diversifying firms (Gorecki, 1975). In other words, entry barriers tend to have more impact on new-firm entry. Based on the theoretical discussions on entry presented above, and in Chapter II, the following proposition emerges:

> *Proposition 5:* The height of entry barriers within an industry will be negatively related to the rate of new venture formation within an industry.

Proposition 5 is illustrated as path B-E in Figure III-1.

Constraints on Exploitation by Existing Firms: Organizational Inertia

The foregoing discussion argues that market opportunities are created by change within an industry. However, the ability of existing firms to take advantage of emerging opportunities may be constrained. The question of whether firms are able to adapt to changes in their organizational environment is a central debate of organization researchers (Astley & Van de Ven, 1983) and has been discussed by organization theorists (Miller & Friesen, 1980), sociologists (Stinchcombe, 1965), economists (Leibenstein, 1979), and others. The current theory builds on recent evidence that organizations are both adaptive and inertial (see Chapter II) and argues that the degree of inertia evidenced by a firm or in an industry can be characterized. If existing firms in an industry are inertial, opportunities not exploited by them will be available to independent entrepreneurs who can exploit the opportunity through the initiation of a venture. This has been implied by a variety of authors, including Penrose (1963), Kirzner (1979), Leibenstein (1979), Winter (1990), and Hannan and Freeman (1984). Thus the following proposition which is illustrated as path C-E in Figure III-1:

Proposition 6: The degree of inertia exhibited by firms within an industry will be positively related to the rate of new venture formation within an industry.

Comparison to Other Discussions of Disequilibrium and Entrepreneurship

In order to position the present model within the larger body of literature on disequilibrium and entrepreneurship, comparisons of the present model to those of other authors is appropriate. The following paragraphs discuss the relation between the present model of entrepreneurship and new venture formation, and other authors' theoretical perspectives on these topics. The comparisons focus on the central aspects of each of the author's theories. The comparison of the present model to that of Schumpeter (1934) is especially interesting, since it represents a contrasting viewpoint in some respects.

Kirzner's (1973, 1979, 1983) approach to the market process is central to the theoretical arguments presented herein. Kirzner suggests that market opportunities are created by changes in the market. Disequilibrium conditions imply the availability of the potential for at least temporary profit-taking. Entrepreneurs react to the availability of profit opportunities by initiating productive activities which address those opportunities. However, the present theory does not assume price to be the only competitive variable (as Kirzner seems to do). Within a system characterized by heterogeneous demand, price is not the only variable which can be modified in order to meet the market opportunities that exist. Changes in tastes and preferences, for example, can be addressed by a new product feature that other producers do not recognize. Kirzner's view of the entrepreneur as an arbitrageur is therefore slightly limiting in that arbitrage implies only buying low and selling high. Given heterogeneous demand and supply possibilities, profit opportunities are much more extensive and complex than that implied by Kirzner.

The most important implication of Leibenstein's (1968, 1979) work for the present model is the recognition that firms are often inertial and are unable to recognize or act upon opportunities within the economic system. Although the present model views inertia somewhat differently than Leibenstein, the basic idea that inertia leads to the persistence of market opportunities is similar. The other contribution of Leibenstein is his recognition that disequilibrium is associated with market opportunities and these "imperfect" markets are related to entrepreneurial activity.

In some respects, Penrose's (1963) theory is similar to the one presented here. First of all, she emphasizes the link between extant opportunities and economic activity. Entrepreneurship is a direct function of the opportunities available in the market. In addition, Penrose recognizes the fundamental factors which result in such opportunities. These are described as the precursors to economic growth. Finally, Penrose touches upon the inertial properties of large organizations and hypothesizes situations whereby the rate of growth in opportunities will exceed the rate at which firms can keep up with them. As such, Penrose recognizes the role of inertial properties of organizations, but treats them in an overly simplistic manner. It is not just the maximum rate of expansion which limits existing firms from exploiting opportunities, it is also a myriad of other factors such as technological capability, diseconomies of scale, specialized assets, and non-maximizing behavior. To be fair, Penrose does recognize other possibilities besides limited growth rates, as evidenced by the following statement: "If growth is accompanied by the creation of important new industries and new technologies which are not in their inception under the control of existing large firms, there will be scope for the entry of new firms . . . ." (Penrose, 1963: 223). However, her cursory treatment of this issue indicates that she does not fully consider the multi-dimensional nature of organizational inertia and the advantages the new entrant firms might thereby have over existing firms.

While Schultz's (1975) study provides an additional verification for the ideas presented herein, it also provides a useful link between theories of entrepreneurial demand and supply. Demand for entrepreneurial ability "is determined by the events that give rise to observed disequilibria and that supply is one of the components of human capital (Schultz, 1975: 827). Gilad (1982) performs a similar link between demand and supply determinants by hypothesizing a relation between Kirzner's (1973) concept of entrepreneurial alertness and internal locus of control.

Schumpeter (1934) views the entrepreneur as the great disequilibrator who upsets the current market equilibrium by introducing new combinations (Schumpeter, 1934). In contrast, the present theory is based upon the Austrian perspective, which sees the entrepreneur as the equilibrator who brings the market closer to a state of equilibrium by exploiting opportunities available in a state of disequilibrium. Sandberg (1986: 32) discusses the issue thus:

> The key insight garnered from the Austrian school's
> theories of entrepreneurship is that the entrepreneur is not
> upsetting an equilibrium state, even when upsetting the
> status quo. Instead, the economy moves toward equilibrium
> to the extent that the entrepreneur correctly anticipates
> future conditions and facilitates other individuals' efforts to
> achieve their own objectives. Disequilibrium is a necessary
> condition for entrepreneurial success, not a consequence of
> it.

Kirzner (1973) argues that the Schumpeterian and Austrian perspectives represent opposing views which are not compatible. The Schumpeterian perspective gives no recognition to the imitative entrepreneur who moves the market to equilibrium. Likewise, Kirzner does not seem to recognize the innovative capacity of the entrepreneur, seeing change in markets as being exogenous to the entrepreneurial role. Recently, Cheah (1990) attempted to reconcile the two perspectives, arguing that the Austrian and Schumpeterian views complement each other. Cheah suggests that the activities of Schumpeterian entrepreneurs (innovators creating disequilibrium and uncertainty) increase the availability of opportunities for Austrian entrepreneurs (imitators moving the market towards equilibrium and certainty). But Cheah's reconciliation requires understanding in further detail the nature of the Schumpeterian and Austrian entrepreneurs. In fact, reconciliation of the two viewpoints requires recognition of the dichotomy in the two perspectives' conceptualization of the entrepreneur and disequilibrium.

To Schumpeter, the essence of the role of the entrepreneur is innovation. The entrepreneur upsets the equilibrium state by introducing new combinations. To Kirzner, on the other hand, the essence of the entrepreneurial role is opportunity-seizing productive activity. Thus, the *imitative* business person is an entrepreneur in Kirzner's world, but not in Schumpeter's. Though he gives innovation little attention, Kirzner would not exclude the *innovative* entrepreneur from his conceptualization. At any rate, the consideration of innovation in the role of the entrepreneur represents a fundamental difference in the two perspectives. Yet, when the role of inventive activity is made explicit, it is possible to see the two perspectives as being compatible.

The fundamental premise that allows reconciliation of the two views is that invention (or innovation) and the initiation of productive activities are *conceptually*, and often empirically, distinct. That is, it is useful to consider the creation of new ideas, methods, etc., and the implementation of them through productive activities as two separate functions. In certain situations, the entrepreneur creates the innovation, and then proceeds to take advantage of it through productive activity. In many other cases, however, the entrepreneur does not perform the innovative activity. For example, the entrepreneur develops products based on others' technological innovations.

At any rate, the important point is that the two functions of invention and entrepreneurship do not always occur simultaneously and should be conceptually distinguished. Thus, innovation is not what makes an entrepreneur. Not all innovators are entrepreneurs, and not all entrepreneurs are innovators. This was exemplified in the writings of Rosen: ". . . Entrepreneurship is not invention. Rather it is exploiting the new opportunities that inventors provide, more in the form of marketing and developing them for widespread use in the economy than developing the knowledge itself. To that extent, one might say that invention is the mother of entrepreneurship" (1983: 307). Conceptually, invention precedes entrepreneurship, which is the application of inventions (Rosen, 1983). Austrian theory suggests that at the moment of invention, the market exists at a state of disequilibrium, with the application of the invention waiting to happen (Kirzner, 1971). Thus, invention itself creates the condition of disequilibrium. Application of that invention to productive activity (entrepreneurship) moves the market closer to equilibrium.

If invention and entrepreneurship are conceived as distinct functions, what does that imply for Schumpeterian and Austrian views of entrepreneurship? Basically, the Austrian concept of the entrepreneur is broader and might be seen as being inclusive of the Schumpeterian entrepreneur. More specifically, the Schumpeterian entrepreneur might be seen as a special case of the Austrian entrepreneur who performs the additional function of innovation. This is illustrated in Figure III-6 below. Circle A in Figure III-6 represents the innovator who, through his/her innovation creates the state of disequilibrium and the opportunities which are then available to entrepreneurs. Circle B represents the entrepreneur as proposed herein (the Austrian entrepreneur). The intersection of the circles A and B is representative of the Schumpeterian entrepreneur who simultaneously performs both the role of the innovator and the role of Austrian entrepreneur.

Schumpeter espoused the narrower view that the two functions occur simultaneously because he was primarily concerned with long-term economic development. His focus on long-term economic growth likely caused him to overlook the possibility that innovative and entrepreneurial activities are distinct functions. The Schumpeterian entrepreneur initiates the underlying industry change that he

Fig. III-6: Conceptualization
of Austrian and Schumpeterian
Entrepreneurs

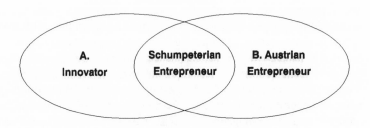

simultaneously exploits through productive activities. This explains why Schumpeter perceived the entrepreneur as the great disequilibrator. He emphasized the innovative activity which creates the state of disequilibrium. And, because this innovative, disequilibrating activity is often strong, Schumpeter did not recognize that the initiation of productive activities represented an opposing force which *begins* the process of equlilibration. Austrian economic theory, and that espoused herein, suggests that at the moment of invention, the market exists at a state of disequilibrium with the application of the invention waiting to happen (Kirzner, 1973). Thus, invention immediately creates the condition of disequilibrium. Application of that invention to productive activity (entrepreneurship) moves the market closer to equilibrium.

In summary, Cheah's proposition that the Schumpeterian and Austrian views are compatible is valid once consideration is given to the distinction between invention and entrepreneurship. The Schumpeterian perspective is appropriate for instances where the entrepreneur performs both the inventive and purely entrepreneurial role. The simultaneous occurrence of these two activities may be common, and the evidence thereof is probably what led Schumpeter to view entrepreneurship in this manner. The Schumpeterian entrepreneur, as well as the non-entrepreneurial inventor, creates the disequilibrium in which opportunities are available to the Austrian entrepreneur. But, the Schumpeterian entrepreneur simultaneously uses his/her innovation to initiate productive activity. In this process he acts as the Austrian entrepreneur, initiating the movement toward equilibrium.

DEVELOPMENT OF TESTABLE HYPOTHESES

Empirical analysis of the propositions presented above required the development of more specific, testable hypotheses. This section translates the general propositions into precise hypotheses. Given the limits of the present study, not all of the propositions presented above will be analyzed. The empirical test will focus on Propositions 4, 5, and 6. These propositions correspond to paths A-E, B-E, and C-E in Figure III-1, respectively. Propositions 1, 2, and 3 concentrate on the more general concept of entrepreneurship as well as on the intermediate variable, market opportunity. Since new venture formation, rather than entrepreneurship, is the focus of the present study, and because of the difficulty in measuring market opportunity, Propositions 1, 2, and 3 will not be not tested herein.

This section proceeds as follows. First, four hypotheses on industry dynamism and new venture formations are developed. Then, the propositions on entry barriers and new venture formation are translated into specific hypotheses. Finally, hypotheses on organizational inertia and new venture formation are developed.

Specific Hypotheses on Industry Dynamism and New Venture Formation

Five types of dynamism were identified in the previous section: increases in demand, modification of demand characteristics, technological development, new sources of supply, and political/ regulatory change. Of these five types, three were used in the empirical investigation: demand growth, modification of demand characteristics, and technological development. They were chosen because they were the most amenable to quantitative measurement. Specific hypotheses for each of these types of dynamism are developed below.

Demand growth. Demand growth has long been viewed as an inducement to entry by researchers in industrial organization economics (Gorecki, 1975, Highfield & Smiley, 1987, Yip, 1982). Theoretically, a growing demand creates a continual opportunity for new firms to serve. In addition, growth in demand will increase potential entrants' profit expectations, since the added capacity of entry will have a less severe effect on industry capacity and prices. Empirical research has consistently supported a positive relationship between industry growth and entry (Harrigan, 1981; Hause & DuReitz, 1984; Duetsch, 1975; Orr, 1974; MacDonald, 1986; Gorecki, 1975; Highfield & Smiley, 1987). These findings and theoretical arguments imply that the greater the industry rate of demand growth, the greater the rate of new venture formation within the industry.

> *Hypothesis 1:* The industry rate of demand growth will be positively related to the number of new venture formations within an industry.

Modification of demand characteristics. The modification of demand characteristics can also impact entrepreneurship and the formation of new ventures. The central idea is that the more the characteristics of demand change, the more opportunities are created for exploitation by new firms. Changes in tastes and preferences modify the nature of the demand and thereby alter the type and quantity of products desired by consumers.

Niche dynamism. One way to to look at modifications of demand characteristics is relative to the concept of industry niches, or sub-industry level demand. Basically, the existence of a large number of niches within an industry may mean that more opportunities are available for new firms to enter. This idea is parallel to that of Porter (1981) who argues that entry into an industry is less difficult for firms who target a specific strategic group (strategic groups have been argued to correspond to niches within a broader market (Hatten & Hatten, 1987)).

However, the most extensive opportunities are created when the niches in an industry are changing. Changes in tastes and preferences can cause an entirely new niche to arise, split a given industry demand into two or more niches, reduce one niche while increasing another, etc. Bedeian and Zammuto (1991) term such dynamics changes in niche shape or niche size, but they can also take the form of creation of an entirely new niche. According to Bedeian and Zammuto, a niche is defined as "a resource space within which organizations can operate and survive" (1991: 361). Niche size is the "level or amount of performance a niche will support" (1991: 362), referring to the number of organizations it will sustain. Niche shape "refers to the ranges or types of activities that a niche's resources will support" (1991: 361). Changes in niche shape and size occur over time according to technological development, government regulation, consumer preferences and other factors. In addition, changes in niche size and shape alter the density of organizations which serve the niche. Where changes in niches result in decreased density, opportunities are said to be created for "entrepreneurs and prospectors" (1991: 366) who can move quickly to take advantage of the changes. Increasing niche size reduces the density of a niche and thereby may create opportunities for the formation of new ventures.

Such arguments relate to increasing demand, but at a dis-aggregated level. Industry-level demand growth may not reflect the variability of demand within the niches in an industry. It is possible that an industry can have zero demand growth, yet have tremendous variability in sales in the niches within an industry. If one niche is growing significantly while another is shrinking, one could view this industry as highly dynamic despite the fact that it is not growing at the industry level. A growing niche could represent an opportunity for a venture regardless of the level of industry growth. Thus, higher niche-level sales dynamism encourages entrepreneurship and new venture formation. Entry through the exploitation of new niches (and growing niches) has been seen as a strategy which can be used to enter industries without facing many of the larger incumbents (Porter, 1980). This analysis implies that the greater the changes in niche size occurring in an industry, the greater the rate of entrepreneurship within the industry. Other things equal:

> *Hypothesis 2*: The dynamism occurring within niches in an industry will be positively related to the number of new venture formations within an industry.

Demand volatility. At a more basic level, the variability of demand over time in an industry may be indicative of the overall dynamism in that industry and thereby related to the formation of new ventures. Organization theorists consider environmental dynamism to be of utmost importance to the design of organizations. In short, the fit between an organization's strategy and structure and the extent of dynamism in its environment is crucial to the success of the organization (See, for example, Bedeian & Zammuto, 1991; Emery & Trist, 1965; Burns & Stalker, 1961). Environmental dynamism, as conceptualized by organization theorists, is also considered to be an important aspect of the unpredictability of organizational environments (Dess & Beard, 1984; Duncan, 1972). In an empirical examination of the concept of environmental dynamism, Dess and Beard (1984) show that instability in industry sales over time is an important contributor to dynamism. Thus, the volatility of industry demand serves as an indicator of the dynamics of organizational environments and should thereby be related to the extent of new venture formations.

> *Hypothesis 3:* The volatility of demand in an industry will be positively related to the number of new venture formations within an industry.

Technological development. A number of authors have proposed that technological development relative to an industry will increase the formation of new firms within that industry. Highfield and Smiley (1987) suggest that technological progress attracts entrants seeking to exploit new products and processes. Acs and Audretsch (1989) view this as a sort of technological opportunity whereby new firms are attracted to pursue such opportunities. Yip (1982) argues that technological change creates market disequilibrium and thereby attracts new entrants. However, other authors have contended that technologically intense industries will have an inherent scale barrier due to the added cost of performing R&D activities (Acs & Audretsch, 1989). Thus, the technological intensity of an industry may have a dual role in the determination of new venture formations. Empirical evidence (See Chapter II) has been mixed, but may indicate that the barrier effect of technological intensity is greater than the technological opportunity effect. Nonetheless, there is theoretical and empirical justification for the validity of either argument.

The present research argues that technological intensity has greater opportunity than barrier effects on new venture formations. Individual entrepreneurs often will find no technological barrier to entry because these entrepreneurs are highly educated and skilled in the technology of the industry entered. This is evidenced in the great number of spin-off entrepreneurs (entrepreneurs that form new ventures after leaving a high-technology firm in the same industry) which have been seen in the electronics and biotechnology industries in recent years (see, for example, Mitton, 1989). Cooper, using different terminology, explicated the role of "incubator organizations" (1985: 75) in the creation of growth-oriented firms. He found that entrepreneurs in technical industries usually start businesses which are related to their previous work experience. Thus, technological entrepreneurs may be able to overcome technological scale barriers due to the fact that they already have knowledge and abilities in the relevant technology. Another factor which aids in overcoming technological barriers to new venture formation is that venture capital plays an important role in promoting the creation of firms seeking technological opportunities (Florida & Kenney, 1988; Timmons & Bygrave, 1986).

While the measurement of technological change remains a fundamental problem in studies of innovation and market structure, research and development intensity is the most commonly used measure of innovative *input* (Cohen & Levin, 1989). Research and development intensity is defined as the total research and development expenditures for all establishments within an industry divided by total industry sales (Hughes, 1988). It is intended to represent the current flow of resources devoted to the generation of innovation within an industry (Cohen & Levin, 1989). Thus, one can argue that the extent of research and development performed by firms in an industry is indicative of the extent of technological development, and that the greater the R&D intensity, the greater the new venture formation within an industry.

> *Hypothesis 4:* An industry's research and development intensity will be positively related to the number of new venture formations within the industry.

Specific Hypotheses on Entry Barriers and New Venture Formation

Proposition 5 proposes that the height of industry entry barriers will be negatively related to the rate of new venture formation in an industry (illustrated by path B-E in Figure III-1). The following paragraphs present specific hypotheses on the relationship between a number of barriers to entry and new venture formation. The entry barriers used in the hypotheses include advertising intensity, economy of scale related barriers (excess capacity and capital requirements), and industry concentration. These were chosen based on theoretical foundations which imply they should have an effect on new venture formations, as well as because of their common usage in the industrial organization economics literature.

Advertising intensity. The role of advertising intensity as a barrier to entry was discussed in Chapter II. Advertising levels are considered a barrier to entry for two reasons. First of all, industry levels of advertising are a contributor to (Bain, 1956), or at the very least an indicator of (Comanor & Wilson, 1967), the extent of product differentiation in an industry. Product differentiation results from differences in the qualities of goods, or in the reputation of a good in the consumer's mind (Gilbert, 1989). Product differentiation is viewed as a barrier to entry by industrial organization economists since it provides advantage to incumbent firms through customer loyalty, superior product design, control of distribution, and switching costs (Gilbert, 1989; Bain, 1956). Bain (1956) argues that product differentiation is the strongest barrier to entry. In this respect, higher advertising associated with product differentiation creates additional selling costs which must be incurred by entrants in order to overcome loyalties and induce customer switching (Comanor & Wilson, 1967).

Advertising intensity also creates a barrier to the establishment of new firms due to the additional capital requirement needed for entry into an industry with high advertising levels. Moreover, since advertising expenditures exhibit economies of scale (Comanor & Wilson, 1967), entry into an industry with high advertising at a less than minimum efficient scale will place the entrant at a cost disadvantage.

These arguments on advertising intensity and entry of new firms into an industry lead to the following hypothesis:

> *Hypothesis 5:* Industry advertising expense will be negatively related to the number of new venture formations within an industry.

Empirical studies on the relation between advertising and entry generally support a negative relation, but have been mixed (see Chapter II). The mixed evidence may support the viability of an alternative argument regarding advertising intensity and new firm creation. Higher advertising may have a heterogeneity effect in that high advertising may indicate more ways that firms can devise strategies which avoid direct competition with existing firms (Yip, 1982). Thus, the extent of product differentiation in an industry may be indicative of the extent of opportunities to avoid direct competition (perhaps by serving niches within the market) and may thereby serve as a gateway to entry (Kunkel & Hofer, 1991). The empirical analysis will shed light upon this potential contradiction to Hypothesis 5.

Excess capacity. High excess capacity in an industry creates a barrier to entry in the following manner. If economies of scale are large relative to total industry sales, the entrance of a large scale firm will increase industry capacity such that industry price levels will decline unless incumbent firms reduce output levels (Scherer & Ross, 1990). In addition, theoretical arguments suggest that incumbent firms may use the creation of excess capacity to signal their willingness to retaliate against entrants. Thus:

Hypothesis 6: Industry excess capacity will be negatively related to the number of new venture formations within an industry.

Capital requirements. Economies of scale serve as a barrier to entry in another manner which Bain referred to as the "absolute-capital-requirement effect" (1956: 55). Where economies of scale are important, the capital needed to enter an industry may be so large such that few founders will be able to secure the required funding without being placed at a capital cost disadvantage. Thus, it is reasonable to assume that new ventures will encounter absolute cost disadvantages resulting from higher capital costs related to capital requirements. Empirical studies have almost unanimously shown a negative relation between capital requirements and entry. This conclusion and the discussion in Chapter II lead to the following hypothesis regarding the impact of capital requirements on new venture formation:

Hypothesis 7: Industry capital requirements will be negatively related to the number of new venture formations within an industry.

Industry concentration. Theoretical discussions have traditionally suggested that high industry concentration results in the ability of incumbent firms to collude in order to thwart the activities of new entrants (Orr, 1974). However, theoretical arguments can also be made for a negative relation between these two variables (Highfield & Smiley, 1987). Small-scale entry into a concentrated industry may go unnoticed (Duetsch, 1975), and may thereby be able to reap the generally higher profits of a concentrated industry (Duetsch, 1975). Nonetheless, the present research takes the more traditional approach and argues that industry concentration will dissuade the formation of new ventures. Thus the following hypothesis:

Hypothesis 8: Industry concentration will be negatively related to the number of new venture formations within an industry.

Specific Hypotheses on Organizational Inertia and New Venture Formation

Proposition 6 states that the degree of inertia exhibited by firms in an industry will be positively related to the rate of new venture formations in an industry (illustrated by path C-E in Figure III-1). The paragraphs below develop a number of hypotheses on the relationship between a number of inertia-producing variables and new venture formations.

Factors which might increase the inertial properties of existing firms in an industry can be classified into two general categories. The first might be viewed as *industry structural* factors which impact the inertial properties of organizations within the industry. The second are *individual-firm* characteristics which result in inertia. Conceptually, these two sources of inertia within an industry are likely to overlap in the sense that inertia-promoting structural factors will lead to greater individual-firm inertia. In order to gauge the extent of industrywide inertia which results from individual-firm inertial characteristics, it is necessary to aggregate individual-firm level factors. In other words, summing the inertial characteristics of firms in an industry should give a measure of the overall level of inertia within the total industry.

A number of individual-firm characteristics may be aggregated to provide an estimation of the overall level of inertia within an industry. Specific factors which have been implied to increase individual firm inertia include the age of the firm (Hannan & Freeman, 1984; Tushman & Romanelli, 1985, Astley, 1985), the size of the firm (Hannan & Freeman, 1984; Tushman & Romanelli, 1985; Keats & Hitt, 1988), and the extent of unionization (Rees, 1962; Addison, 1984; Bemmels, 1987).

Organizational age. The idea that inertial properties increase with the age of a firm is supported by a number of theoretical perspectives. The first relates to ideas on the reliability and accountability of organizations (Hannan & Freeman, 1984; Tushman & Romanelli, 1985) and is exemplified in a statement by Singh, House, and Tucker (1986: 588):

> As organizations grow older, reproducibility of structure, and therefore structural inertia, increases, because organizational members take time to learn to trust and cooperate with each other, learn to coordinate roles (Stinchcombe, 1965), and learn organization-specific skills and routines (Nelson & Winter, 1982).

The second perspective emanates from community ecology and considers the increasing web of acceptance of traditional ways of performing activities in populations of organizations (Astley, 1985; Romanelli, 1989). The third concerns imprinting at founding and the effect that the passage of time has on the dichotomy between the initial strategies and structures and environmental conditions (Stinchcombe, 1965; Boeker, 1989). These three theoretical perspectives on organizational age and inertia are discussed below.

The previous chapter discusses the relationship between an organization's need for reliability and accountability and inertia. In short, organizational reliability and accountability are seen as integral to reproducibility and success, but create resistance to change (Hannan & Freeman, 1984). In addition, accountability and reliability tend to increase with age. This is due to the fact that organizational routines are easier to repeat than create initially and that organization members acquire organization-specific skills (Hannan & Freeman, 1984). While this allows reproducibility to increase with age it is also causes structural inertia to increase with age (Hannan & Freeman, 1984). Similarly, Tushman and Romanelli argue that inertia is time dependent. More specifically, they state that longer convergent periods are associated with increased complexity since "the passage of time permits increased elaboration of values, beliefs, and ideologies at individual, group and organization levels of analysis (Tushman & Romanelli, 1985: 192). Thus, as time passes, the structure and strategy of the organization are self-reinforced and thereby become entrenched and difficult to change.

These ideas fit quite well with researchers' arguments about the nature of bureaucratic organizations. Bureaucracies are seen as useful means for increasing efficiency in organizational operations, but often engender dysfunction through the displacement of goals and resistance to change (Blau, 1956). The characteristics of bureaucracy: specialization, hierarchy of authority, a system of rules, and impersonality (Blau, 1956) are parallel to the ideas of reliability and accountability discussed above and could also be reasonably predicted to increase with the age of an organization.

Justification for a positive relation between the age of firms and inertia can also be found in the community ecology perspective. Thoughts discussed by Astley (1985) and Romanelli (1989) suggest that organizational communities become more inertial as they evolve over time to a condition of closure. Communities of populations are "functionally integrated systems of interacting populations" (Astley, 1985: 234) having an interdependence which increases over time to the point that they actually shut out influences from the environment (Astley, 1985). This closure is seen as a situation where the community of populations is unable to alter activity patterns. As a result, the increasing age of populations of communities results in a situation whereby new organizations are more likely to introduce variety. Astley sees this as a punctuation of disequilibrium whereby the community disintegrates due to its inertia, and environmental space opens for the creation of new organizations (1985).

A number of researchers have argued that organizations are imprinted by the social conditions existing at the time of the founding, and that the structural characteristics imprinted at this time tend to persist throughout the life of the organization (Stinchcombe, 1965; Boeker, 1988; Boeker, 1989). Thus, "organizations are set on a course at founding from which change may be costly or difficult" and "early patterns of organizing also set boundaries on the range of strategic actions that are likely to be successful for the organization" (Boeker, 1988: 51). If it is true that organizational structures and strategies are imprinted at founding, the gap between an organization's fit with its dynamic environment will continually increase over time. The longer an organization exists, the greater will be the dichotomy between the organization and its environment. This supports the idea that the age of a firm will be linked to its inability to match the needs of its environment and implies that older firms will be less likely to move toward existing opportunities.

According to the above perspectives on reliability and accountability, community ecology, and imprinting, one would expect inertia to be associated with the age of firms. Thus, industries with older firms will exhibit greater inertia than industries with younger firms and:

> *Hypothesis 9:* The age of firms within an industry will be positively related to the number of new venture formations within an industry.

Organizational size. Researchers have also postulated a relationship between the size of firms and organizational inertia. Hannan & Freeman (1984) consider smaller firms to be much more responsive to environmental change since smaller organizations are essentially extensions of individuals. This conclusion is based on the assumption that individuals are able to respond to environmental changes more quickly than organizations. Overall, Hannan & Freeman argue that the speed and flexibility of operations tend to diminish with increasing size. Similarly, Tushman & Romanelli (1985) argue that increased size leads to increased differentiation and specialization of sub-units, increased complexity of systems and structures, and greater formalization and control. This results in greater efficiency, but also reduces the organization's ability to handle new situations and increases the organization's resistance to change. "The larger the organization, the greater its structural complexity and interdependence, and the greater the emphasis on incremental as opposed to discontinuous change" (Tushman & Romanelli, 1985: 192). Bureaucracy research has also suggested that the problems associated with the administration of large organizations lead to bureaucratization (Blau, 1956). A number of characteristics associated with bureaucracies may inhibit organizational adaptability including dysfunctional learning behavior (March & Simon, 1958), resistance to change (Blau, 1956), and goal displacement (Merton, 1949).

In addition, organization size has been related to a number of organizational structural characteristics which may increase inertia. A study by Pugh, Hickson, Hinings, and Turner (1969) shows that organizational size has an important causal effect on a number of structural characteristics. Research by Blau & Schoenherr (1971) has shown that organization size increases differentiation and formalization, and Dean and Snell (1991) suggest that these variables decrease the ability of organizations to change. In addition, other organization theorists (Chandler, 1962; Downs, 1967) have suggested that larger organizations have difficulty adapting to environmental change (Dean & Snell, 1991). Using many of these arguments as a foundation, two recent empirical studies use organizational size as a measure of inertia (Keats & Hitt; 1988; Dean & Snell, 1991).

In short, a positive relationship is expected between firm size and organizational inertia, and between the size of firms in an industry and the inertia within that industry. Thus:

> *Hypothesis 10:* The size of firms within an industry will be positively related to the number of new venture formations within an industry.

Extent of unionization. The debate over the effect of unions on organizations and the economy has continued for some time. (See, for example, Rees, 1962.) Many empirical studies on the effects of unionism have often concentrated on the relationship between unionism and labor productivity (Flanagan, 1990). Recent research has shown a consistent, positive relationship between unionism and labor productivity

(Flanagan, 1990). Yet, despite the positive productivity effect, managers consistently try to avoid unionization of operations (Flanagan, 1990; Freeman & Medhoff, 1979b). Various reasons can be offered to explain this paradox (Flanagan, 1990). The first and most obvious concerns the wage effects of unionism. Considerable evidence exists that union workers receive a significant wage premium (about 10 to 15 percent) over non-union workers (Flanagan, 1990). Thus, the wage effects of unionism may offset the productivity effects (Freeman & Medhoff, 1979b; Flanagan, 1990). However, this, in itself, is probably not enough to explain managers' tendency to attempt to avoid unionization. Another possible explanation is that unions impede the adaptive ability of organizations (Flanagan, 1990). In other words unions may encourage organizational inertia by impeding organizations' ability to react to technological developments, demand modifications, and other industry changes.

The most simplistic of arguments for the negative impact of unionism on adaptive ability relates to restrictive work rules such as manning requirements, work pace standards, and seniority-based promotions (Flanagan, 1990). Rees (1962) suggests that unions may resist attempts to change obsolete work rules and that changing long standing work rules is extremely difficult in a unionized environment. In addition, work rules often evolve into "featherbedding" situations whereby old work rules are kept in order to perpetuate work positions (Addison, 1984). Freeman and Medhoff (1979b) offer the counterargument that the collective bargaining process in unionized firms facilitates worker-management communication and thereby increases the potential for organizational change. However, it is likely that the types of change encouraged by unions are incremental changes in operations rather than adaptive strategic changes. Other authors have argued that unions have a negative impact on the flexibility management possesses in reacting to environmental change. Bemmels (1987) states that organizational flexibility in responding to technological or demand changes may be inhibited by vigorous union opposition. Flanagan (1990) framed this problem as an agent-principle issue. He implies that union motivated gains in productivity may actually inhibit organizational adaptability since an over-emphasis on productivity constrains managerial discretion. Finally, Kochan, McKersie, and Cappelli (1984) argue that highly unionized firms will be limited in their ability to pursue non-union strategic options. Although theoretical arguments have presented a valid case for the inertial effects of unions on organizations, empirical evidence on a link between unionism and organizational adaptability is unavailable.

In sum, unions may reduce adaptability through restrictive work rules, and general opposition to change. Much of the opposition to change may be motivated by a principle-agent goal dichotomy. The above discussion on unionization and organizational adaptive ability implies that industries with more unionization will exhibit greater existing-firm inertia, and:

> *Hypothesis 11:* The extent of industry unionization will be positively related to the number of new venture formations within an industry.

Acs and Audretsch (1989) verify the positive unionism-entry relationship in a study of entry in U.S. manufacturing industries. They find that the percentage of union employees in an industry is positively associated with the entry of small firms.

THEORETICAL SUMMARY

The central theoretical argument of the present research can be summarized as follows (See Figure III-1 for an illustration of the conceptual model and Figure III-7 below for an illustration of the empirical model). Changes in markets create a state of disequilibrium whereby the needs of consumers are not perfectly matched to the offerings of producers. Market dynamism can take several forms, including changes in the nature and size of demand, changes in technologies (product and process), new sources of supply, and changes in political/regulatory conditions. Disequilibrium, somewhat by definition, is characterized by the existence of market opportunities for alert entrepreneurs to exploit for economic gain. Generally, the greater the extent of change, and the greater the unpredictability of that change, the greater will be the extent of disequilibrium created, and the more market (or entrepreneurial) opportunities are created.

Various economic actors will move to exploit the market opportunities which are created by market dynamism. These actors can be either existing firms or new ventures. Although movement towards extant opportunities by any of these actors can be termed entrepreneurship, new venture creation is the focus of the present research. The issue is to what extent new firms will be able to take advantage of the opportunities associated with a state of disequilibrium. The rate of new venture creation within an industry is a function of the

Fig. III-7: Empirical Model of New Venture Formation

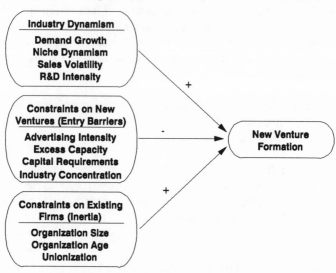

constraints on existing firms and the constraints on new venture formations. Organizational inertia constrains existing firms from exploiting market opportunities, while entry barriers constrain the emergence of new ventures within an industry.

In short, the greater the change in a market, the greater the market opportunities created and the further the market is moved from an equilibrium state. More market opportunities imply more potential for entrepreneurial activity. Industry barriers to entry and the inertial properties of existing firms determine the extent to which new ventures will exploit available market opportunities.

A number of propositions and hypotheses regarding industry dynamism, entry barriers, and organizational inertia, and new venture formation have been proposed. More specifically, demand growth, demand volatility, niche dynamism, and research and development intensity are important aspects of industry dynamism and are proposed to be positively related to new venture formation. Four entry barriers, advertising intensity, capital requirements, capacity utilization, and industry concentration are expected to have a negative impact on new venture formation. The age, size, and extent of unionization of firms within an industry are proposed to encourage inertia and thereby increase new venture formations.

IV

RESEARCH DESIGN AND METHODOLOGY

Chapter Overview

This chapter describes the research design used to test the new venture formations model presented in Chapter III. It begins with a description of the research design and the regression model and a review of the specific hypotheses tested. Then, a description of the sample of manufacturing industries is presented. Finally, the various data sources are explained, and the model variables presented.

REGRESSION MODEL, HYPOTHESES, AND RESEARCH METHOD

Regression Model

The general functional form of the model developed in Chapter III is provided below in Equation IV-1, and more specifically in Equation IV-2. The three conceptual variables examined include industry dynamism, entry barriers, and organizational inertia. Market dynamism was operationalized through percent sales growth, niche dynamism, sales volatility, and research and development intensity. Entry barriers analyzed include advertising intensity, excess capacity, the logarithm of capital requirements, and the four-firm industry concentration ratio. Organizational inertia was operationalized as the weighted average age of firms, average size of firms, and extent of unionization.

Equation IV-1: New Venture Formation = F (Industry Dynamism, Entry Barriers, Organizational Inertia)

Equation IV-2: New Venture Formation = F (Sales Growth, Niche Dynamism, Sales Volatility, Research and Development Intensity, Excess Capacity, Concentration, Advertising Intensity, Capital Requirements, Unionization, Age of Firms, Size of Firms)

The conceptual model of new venture formation was tested with standard multiple linear regression. All independent variables were entered on the same step. The complete regression model is given in Equation IV-3.

The model is specified in semi-logarithmic form for most variables. New venture formations are transformed logarithmically. All of the dependent variables, except for capital requirements, have not been logarithmically transformed. This model specification follows that of other authors (Orr, 1974; Khemani & Shapiro, 1986; Shapiro & Khemani, 1987) and was chosen for the following reasons. Most importantly, the semi-logarithmic specification creates a model where the relationships between the variables are in percentage terms (Orr, 1974). The only variables not in percentage terms as initially gathered are capital requirements, weighted average age of firms, and average size of firms. Capital requirements were logarithmically transformed, thereby maintaining the percentage/percentage interpretation for this relation. For firm size and age, however, logarithmic transformations were not deemed appropriate. No prior evidence of a percentage/percentage relationship existed, and no justification was evident for implying that a percentage/percentage relationship would be appropriate. Another justification for the semi-logarithmic form is that "it allows an implicit interaction among the independent variables" (Khemani & Shapiro, 1986: 1245). This mitigates the need to specify interaction terms within the model (Khemani & Shapiro, 1986). Finally, empirical examination of the the non-logarithmically transformed dependent variable reveals that it is highly skewed (the results of this examination are presented in Chapter V). Logarithmic transformation of positively skewed variables acts to eliminate skewness and thereby creates a distribution which is much closer to normal and has less extreme outliers. In sum, the model has been specified in a semi-logarithmic form by taking the logarithm of the dependent variable, but leaving most of the independent variables untransformed.

$$\text{LOGNVF}_{\text{sum}(77\text{-}78,79\text{-}80),i} = b_0 + b_1\text{PCTGRTH}_{72\text{-}78,i} + b_2\text{NICHEDYN}_{72\text{-}77,i}$$

$$+ \; b_3\text{VOL}_{72\text{-}78,i} + b_4\text{RD}_{\text{ave}(76,77),i} + b_5\text{ADV}_{\text{ave}(76,77),i}$$

$$+ \; b_6\text{EXCAP}_{\text{ave}(76,77),i} + b_7\text{LOGCR}_{76,i} + b_8\text{C4}_{77,i} + b_9\text{WTDAGE}_{78,i}$$

$$+ \; b_{10}\text{SZ}_{78,i} + b_{11}\text{UNION}_{68\text{-}72,i} + e_i$$

Where:
New Venture Formation
    LOGNVF = Logarithm of Number of New Venture Formations

Industry Dynamism
    PCTGRTH = Percentage Annual Sales Growth
    NICHEDYN = Niche Dynamism
    VOL = Sales Volatility
    RD = R&D Intensity

Entry Barriers
    ADV = Advertising Intensity
    EXCAP = Excess Capacity
    LOGCR = Log of Capital Requirements
    C4 = Four-Firm Concentration Ratio

Organizational Inertia
    WTDAGE = Weighted Average Age of Firms in the Industry
    SZ = Average Size of Establishments in the Industry
    UNION = Extent of Industry Unionization

    i = 4-digit S.I.C. Industry

EQUATION IV-3: REGRESSION MODEL

Hypotheses

The individual hypotheses associated with the regression model are shown in Table IV-1. The table provides the null and alternative

TABLE IV-1: HYPOTHESES

Industry Dynamism

Hypothesis 1: Percent Sales Growth (PCTGRTH)
H_0: $b_1 <= 0$
H_a: $b_1 > 0$

Hypothesis 2: Niche Dynamism (NICHEDYN)
H_0: $b_2 <= 0$
H_a: $b_2 > 0$

Hypothesis 3: Sales Volatility (VOL)
H_0: $b_3 <= 0$
H_a: $b_3 > 0$

Hypothesis 4: R&D Intensity (RD)
H_0: $b_4 <= 0$
H_a: $b_4 > 0$

Entry Barriers

Hypothesis 5: Advertising Intensity (ADV)
H_0: $b_5 >= 0$
H_a: $b_5 < 0$

Hypothesis 6: Excess Capacity (EXCAP)
H_0: $b_6 >= 0$
H_a: $b_6 < 0$

Hypothesis 7: Log of Capital Requirements (LOGCR)
H_0: $b_7 >= 0$
H_a: $b_7 < 0$

Hypothesis 8: Four-Firm Concentration Ratio (C4)
H_0: $b_8 >= 0$
H_a: $b_8 < 0$

Organizational Inertia

Hypothesis 9: Weighted Average Age of Firms (WTDAGE)
H_0: $b_9 <= 0$
H_a: $b_9 > 0$

Hypothesis 10: Average Size of Establishments (SZ)
H_0: $b_{10} <= 0$
H_a: $b_{10} > 0$

Hypothesis 11: Extent of Unionization (UNION)
H_0: $b_{11} <= 0$
H_a: $b_{11} > 0$

hypotheses as developed in Chapter III, and translates those hypotheses into predicted regression coefficient directions. The analysis seeks to either reject or accept the null hypotheses.

Similar to a study by Shapiro and Khemani (1987), it was assumed that new venture formations respond to determinants after a lag. Thus, the independent variables were lagged relative to the measure of new venture formation. The pre-formation period in which the independent variables were measured was 1972 to 1978. Decisions on the specific period of lags are shown in Equation IV-1 and are further described in each of the variable descriptions. The following factors were taken into consideration when determining the lagged structure. The most limiting constraint was data availability. Some lag periods were restricted by the source of data used. A second factor was how long it might take entrepreneurs to establish productive capacity after noting the availability of a market opportunity. Harrigan (1981, 1983a) suggested that one year was an appropriate period. It was necessary to consider a third factor in setting the lag period. Brown and Phillips (1989) stated that it takes two to four years, on average, for a new firm to show up in the USEEM/USELM database. However, the time it takes for manufacturing firms to enter is probably much less than the average, since they are more likely to require immediate credit. Due to this uncertainty in the database and the suggestion of Harrigan (1981,1983a), the dependent variable was measured over a relatively long period (1976-1980), and lags set appropriately.

Research Method

Analysis of the data proceeded in the following manner. First, data from the various sources were compiled into a single file. All entered data values were double checked to insure that no entry errors were made. Next, tests were performed relative to the assumptions of least squares estimators. The dependent variable was then regressed on the twelve independent variables. Standardized and un-standardized regression coefficients and the adjusted R^2 were examined relative to the proposed hypotheses. An F-test was performed to see if a significant relationship existed between the independent and dependent variables. One-tailed t-tests were performed on each of the slope coefficients.

SAMPLE DESCRIPTION

The model was tested using a large sample of U.S. manufacturing industries. New venture formation was measured from 1976 to 1980, and the independent variables were lagged appropriately. Availability of secondary data restricted the possibility of performing the analysis in more recent years.

In 1977, 449 manufacturing industries existed at the four-digit level. The final sample size was reduced due to the existence of some nonhomogeneous industries and missing data. Of these 449, fifteen industries were not included in the sample since, by definition, they were not homogeneous. These fifteen industry classifications are used by the Department of Commerce to classify establishments which do not fit into any other three- or four-digit S.I.C. Thus, they represent a mixture of establishments which are "not elsewhere classified." One example of such an industry is S.I.C. 3499, "Fabricated Metal Products, Not Elsewhere Classified." This industry contains establishments which are appropriately classified under the two digit S.I.C. 34, but do not fit within one of the more specific three- or four-digit categorizations. Thus, it was not appropriate to assume that these classifications represented a single market, and they were not included in the analysis. After the fifteen not elsewhere classified industries were removed from the sample, 434 industries remained. An attempt was made to analyze all of these 434 manufacturing industries, but missing data values eliminated a number of additional cases from the sample. Fifty-two more of the cases dropped out of the sample, resulting in a sample size of 382 industries. This represented 87.8 percent of the 434 (449 minus 15) industries.

Since the sample was not randomly drawn, it was appropriate to compare the cases selected to those not included in the sample. Table IV-2 shows the results of t-tests between the non-sample cases and the sample cases. The tests reveal that some significant differences in the means of the model variables exist. For example, the average number of new venture formations was larger for the sample than for the unused cases (118 vs. 52 average new venture formations). Moreover, the sample industries had a higher percentage annual sales growth rate then the non-sample group (4.2% vs 3.5%). Sales volatility, research and development intensity and four-firm concentration were lower for the sample group (.013 vs. .017, 1.082% vs. 1.453%, and 37.7% vs. 47.9%, respectively). Finally, the average firm size of the

TABLE IV-2: SAMPLE VS. NON-SAMPLE
COMPARISON

Variable	Sample Mean (n=382)	Non-Sample Mean	t
NVF	235.634	106.711 (n=52)	1.80*
PCTGRTH	4.225	3.540 (n=50)	2.20**
VOL	0.013	0.016 (n=50)	-2.57***
RD	1.082	1.453 (n=37)	-1.72*
NICHEDYN	3.245	1.774 (n=37)	1.86*
EXCAP	26.217	27.714 (n=35)	-0.82
C4	37.654	48.298 (n=47)	-3.38***
ADV	1.610	1.733 (n=36)	-0.32
LOGCR	2.929	2.899 (n=51)	0.32
UNION	45.597	44.756 (n=45)	0.30
WTDAGE	39.270	41.732 (n=51)	-0.84
SZ	201.645	601.728 (n=52)	-3.55***

  * Significance <=.1 (two-tailed)
 ** Significance <=.05 (two-tailed)
*** Significance <=.01 (two-tailed)

sample industries was less than half that of non-sample group (202 vs. 592). In short, the sample group contained industries with higher percentage sales growth, lower sales volatility, higher sub-industry level sales variations, lower research and development intensity, lower concentration, smaller firms, and more new venture formations.

The sample/non-sample differences described above are of considerable concern when discussing the applicability of the results to all manufacturing industries. The pattern of some of the differences is partially explained by the source of the missing data values. Neither the Census of Manufactures nor the FTC Line of Business Data reports data values for highly concentrated industries where published data could reveal specific company information. As a result, the sample does not include many of the highly concentrated industries. The bias toward less concentrated industries accounts for the difference in the average firm size between the sample industries and the non-sample industries. Since industry concentration is considered an entry barrier, this bias may also account for the difference between the average number of new venture formations in the two groups.

The implication of the above discussion is that researchers need to be careful when generalizing from the results of this study. While a large portion of the total population of manufacturing industries was included in the study, those industries excluded were unique in certain aspects. Most importantly, the results may not be generalizable to highly concentrated industries.

DATA SOURCES

Secondary data sources were used to operationalize the variables in the study. The data sources used included the U.S. Small Business Administration's (SBA) U.S. Establishment Longitudinal Microdata file (USELM), the Federal Trade Commission's (FTC) Line of Business Data, Freeman and Medhoff's (1979) estimates of unionization, and the U.S. Department of Commerce's Census of Manufactures, Annual Survey of Manufactures, and Survey of Plant Capacity. The superior data on research and development and advertising available from the Line of Business Data motivated the use of 1978 and 1980 as the base years of analysis. The SBA USELM files, the Census of Manufactures,the Annual Survey of Manufactures, and the FTC Line of Business Data are discussed below.

Data Source Compatibility

During the process of building the datafile, compatibility of S.I.C. codes across sources was examined. The 1972 Standard Industrial Classification Manual was used as a guide to the yearly changes in S.I.C. codes. Relatively few four-digit S.I.C. categorizations changed over the period of the study. Where changes did occur, and/or incompatibilities could not be mitigated, the industry was eliminated from the sample. Matching S.I.C.'s across data sources was not generally problematic, as most sources followed the S.I.C. system quite well. Two areas that did present a challenge were with Freeman and Medhoff's (1979a) unionization data and the FTC Line of Business Data. The specific methodologies used with these data sources will be discussed shortly.

SBA USEEM/USELM File

The U.S. Establishment and Enterprise Microdata file (USEEM) and U.S. Establishment and Enterprise Longitudinal Microdata file (USELM) was constructed by the Small Business Administration from data provided by Dun & Bradstreet (D&B). D&B collects data on firms and establishments as part of its credit reporting services. This data is aggregated into the Dun's Markets Identifier file, which was then leased to the SBA. The SBA performed extensive editing to ensure the file's accuracy (Brown & Phillips, 1989) and used the data to help understand the impact of public policy on small businesses. The USEEM file provided reliable yearly data on the U.S. establishment population but was inappropriate for longitudinal analysis. The USELM file, a stratified random sample from the USEEM data, was constructed to eliminate the problems inherent in the USEEM data. As a result, the USELM was appropriate for use in longitudinal studies and thereby provided a reliable source of data on establishment starts. Unfortunately, the SBA has now discontinued maintenance of the USELM and USEEM database.

The USEEM file was used to provide data on weighted average age of firms and average size of firms. The USELM file provided the data on new venture formations. Despite a number of disadvantages inherent in the USELM database, it was chosen for a number of reasons. The discussion below provides a brief description of the file and discusses some of the advantages and disadvantages of its use for the present study.

First, the USELM data were chosen because they are probably the best source of data on new business starts which are national in scope and broken down by four-digit S.I.C. Unemployment insurance data (ES202) are collected by four-digit S.I.C. and recorded for all states, but would be nearly impossible to collect at a national level (Birley, 1984). Establishment start data can be obtained from the Census of Manufactures data, but this is only reported every five years and are not as readily available. On the other hand, the USELM database is readily accessible. Finally, use of the database for estimating business starts has a precedent in the literature (see, for example, MacDonald, 1986; Acs & Audretsch, 1989; Highfield & Smiley, 1987).

Despite these crucial advantages of using the USELM file for the present study, the database is not without its limitations. USELM data has been argued to be somewhat untimely, incomplete in certain areas, and sometimes inaccurate. Birley (1984) compared the DMI data (upon which USELM is based) to the ES202 data for an Indiana county. She found that, overall, the DMI files identified only 22 percent of the firms that the ES202 files did. In a more recent study, Aldrich, Kalleberg, Marsden, and Cassell (1989) achieved more positive results regarding the completeness of the DMI file. Their results showed that 42 percent of the new businesses in their sample from the ES202 files were found in the DMI file. While the 22 percent and 42 percent figures seem alarmingly low, they must be taken in context. The USELM file is known for its incompleteness in industries that do not seek out the services of D&B, because firms or establishments enter the database only when they apply for credit or try to obtain insurance (Brown & Phillips, 1989). Consequently, retail and service firms are often under-represented in the database. Fortunately, the problem is not nearly so severe in manufacturing industries. In contrast to Birley's (1984) finding of 22 percent overall completeness, she showed that the USELM data were 55 percent complete in manufacturing. In short, problems of incompleteness in the USEEM file are least severe in manufacturing industries.

The USELM file has also been criticized for its lack of timeliness (Birley, 1984; Aldrich, et. al., 1989). The primary difficulty with the database's timeliness results from the fact that firms do not always appear as soon as they are formed. On average, it takes two to four years after a firm has been created for it to appear in the USELM file (Brown & Phillips, 1989). This is because firms do not always need credit or insurance at initial start-up. The problem is especially severe for retail & service firms (Brown & Phillips, 1989), but may not be as extensive for manufacturing firms since they are more likely to need borrowed funds to cover initial capital expenses. In addition, the issue of timeliness is not as problematic for this study since formation rates have been measured over a fairly long period (four years), and have been lagged behind measures of the independent variables.

Finally, some questions have been raised regarding the accuracy of the database. This criticism has centered around the question of whether firms listed as new businesses are new or whether they have merely changed names, legal status, or ownership (Birley,

1984; Reynolds, West, & Finch, 1985). However, Reynolds et al. (1985) found that 74.1 percent of the manufacturing firms which were listed as new in the DMI file were actually new businesses. In addition, a large portion of the remaining 25.9 percent were not included as "new" by Reynolds et al. because they could not be contacted. Therefore, the accuracy of the data on new firms was probably even higher than the reported 74.1 percent. Aldrich et al. (1989) showed that even a higher percentage (85 percent) of the independent new firms listed in the DMI file were confirmed to be such. Aldrich et al. concluded that most firms identified as new in the DMI file were new businesses.

In summary, the USELM database is the most appropriate database for the present study since it reports new business starts nationally by four-digit S.I.C. In addition, the criticisms it has received have been shown to be much less severe for manufacturing industries.

Department of Commerce Census and Annual Survey of Manufactures

The Department of Commerce performs a census of manufactures every five years. The Annual Survey of Manufactures is based on a sample of firms from the census. The census and survey provide industry structural data such as concentration, payroll, value added, and value of shipments. The data is reported by establishment and then aggregated to four-digit S.I.C industries. In this study, the census and survey data were used for measures of capital requirements, industry concentration, sales growth, and niche dynamism.

FTC Line of Business Data

The FTC Line of Business Data (LBD) were used to provide estimates of research and development intensity and advertising intensity. The LBD report is one of the few sources of data on these variables. The data are reported for lines of business rather than for four-digit S.I.C.'s. While some lines of business correspond to a single four-digit S.I.C. industry, others correspond to groups of four-digit industries. Thus, there are 261 lines of business in the FTC dataset as compared to approximately 449 four-digit industries in the census and USELM data. Since the LBD dataset does not directly correspond to four-digit industries, the values for a particular line of business were assigned to all the four-digit industries contained within that line of business. The FTC provides a cross-reference table which delineates the four-digit S.I.C.'s contained within each line of business. For example, line of business 20.01 is inclusive of two four-digit industries: 2011 and 2013. The value for total R&D in line of business 20.01 is 0.1 percent. Thus for the present study, the R&D intensity assigned to industries 2011 and 2013 was 0.1 percent.

In addition, a number of values were missing in the FTC data. When available, data from other years were substituted for missing values. When other year's data were not available, and where it was deemed appropriate, two or three-digit S.I.C. average values were substituted for the missing values. However, missing cases seeming not to correspond to the other industries in their respective two- or three-digit categories were not assigned an average value, but were left missing.

VARIABLE MEASURES

New Venture Formation

Since new firm entrants are equivalent to new venture formations within an industry, discussions of measures of industry entry are relevant to the issue of how to measure new venture formations. The paragraphs below present a comparison of various means of measuring entry and discuss the implications for a measure of new venture formations.

Authors have discussed the various merits of different measures of industry entry rates. Some authors have used net entry rate (Duetsch, 1975; McGuckin, 1972) while others have deemed gross entry rate to be more appropriate (Hamilton, 1985). Net entry rate captures both entry and exit, since it is a measure of the change in the number of independent firms operating in the industry (Duetsch, 1975). Gross entry rates is more appropriate for this study, since the dissertation focuses on new venture formation and is not concerned with exits as a dependent variable or with the changes in the absolute number of firms in the industry.

Authors have also argued that the size of entrants is important for measuring entry rates since the simple number of firms does not serve as a good indicator of the potential effect that those entrants have on the industry (McGuckin, 1972; Duetsch, 1975). Hause and du Rietz (1984) addressed this difficulty by considering the market shares attained by entrants. For the present study, however, measures of entry which consider size of the entrant are inappropriate, since the primary focus is on the creation of new ventures, not on the effect of those firms on the industry.

The measure of new venture formations (LOGNVF) to be used in the study is the logarithm of the number of new-firm formations from 1976 to 1980. This variable measures the number of new, independent establishments appearing in an industry. A new establishment is recognized by the appearance of a new Dun's DMI number in the USELM database. An establishment receives a Dun's number when it first submits a credit report. The USELM database reports new-firm formations every other year. Thus, this variable was calculated as the sum of the USELM 1978 and 1980 figures. Summing the 1978 and 1980 figures covers four years of new venture formations. The four-year period was chosen for two reasons. First of all, a longer period helped eliminate any anomalies in this variable. Second, this methodology helped mitigate the effect of the lag period for when a firm is actually formed and when it enters into the USELM database. Justification for logarithmically transforming this variable was provided above. Since one of the cases had zero new venture formations, it was necessary to add a small value (0.01) to the NVF variable before taking the logarithm.

Industry Dynamism

The measures of industry dynamism used in the study include percent sales growth, sales volatility, niche dynamism, and research and development intensity.

Sales growth (PCTGRTH). Industry sales growth was measured as the approximate annual percentage increase in industry value of shipments from 1972 to 1978. This was calculated as 100 multiplied by the regression coefficient of the trend in the logarithm (base 10) of value of shipments from 1972 to 1978. The regression equation used to calculate this variable is given below in Equation IV-4. In a few cases where all seven years of data were not available, six years of data were used to calculate the coefficient. If the regression coefficient were calculated without taking the logarithm, the resultant slope would not be comparable across industries. Taking the logarithm of sales transforms the resultant regression coefficient into a measure of the percentage growth and thereby allows comparisons across industries. Dess and Beard (1984) solved this problem by dividing the non-log slope coefficient by the average value of sales over the relevant years. However, the present method of taking the logarithm prior to regressing sales over time is more direct and easily interpretable. The Census of Manufactures and Annual Survey of Manufactures were used as the sources for this measure.

$$Log_{10}(S_{it}) = b_0 + b_1 t + e_i$$

Where:
S = Value of industry shipments in year t
t = Years (1972 to 1978, inclusive)
i = Four-digit S.I.C. industry

EQUATION IV-4: REGRESSION OF LOG OF SHIPMENTS OVER TIME

Niche dynamism (NICHEDYN). Using five-digit S.I.C. categorizations, this variable focuses on changes in sub-industry level demand. Within the Department of Commerce's S.I.C. system, four-digit industries are further classified into five-digit product classes. A given industry can be entirely homogeneous (according to Department of Commerce definition) and have only one product class, or may have more than ten product classes.

The purpose of the NICHEDYN variable was to measure the changes in product classes within an industry. In short, an industry can have tremendous variability in sales within its product classes, yet have zero sales growth at the four-digit level. This variable was devised to reflect the sales dynamism within product classes and was calculated as follows. Based on 1972 value of shipments, the largest product class in the industry was identified. Next, the sales share (relative to the entire industry sales) of this product class was calculated for both 1972 and 1977. Then, the product share in 1972 was subtracted from the product share in 1977. The absolute value of the resultant figure was then taken. If the industry had only one product class in 1972 it was assigned a value of zero for the NICHEDYN variable. The equation used to calculate this variable is given below. The variable is expressed as a percentage. The source of the data was the 1982 Census of Manufactures.

$$NICHEDYN_i = /PRDSHR_{i,77} - PRDSHR_{i,72}/$$

If the number of product classes in 1972 equals one,
NICHEDYN=0

Where:
PRDSHR = Percentage share of total industry sales
accounted for by the largest 1972 product class
i = Four-digit S.I.C. industry

EQUATION IV-5: CALCULATION OF NICHE DYNAMISM

Sales volatility (VOL). Demand volatility was measured as the standard error of the estimate for the regression of the logarithm of value of shipments from 1972 to 1978, divided by average of the logarithm of value of shipments over the same period. Dividing by the average log value of sales allows comparability of this measure across industries. The regression used as the basis for this measure was given in Equation IV-4.

The standard error of the estimate can be interpreted as the estimate of the population's standard deviation of the residuals (Kim & Kohout, 1975; Cohen & Cohen, 1983). It represents the proportion of the Y values (industry sales) that are not associated with the X values (time) (Cohen & Cohen, 1983). Thus, the standard error of the estimate measures the unpredictability of sales over time, and is indicative of the data's dispersion about the trend line.

Although suggested as an appropriate measure of environmental instability by Dess and Beard (1984), the standard error of the *regression coefficient* was not judged to be a good measure of sales volatility for the present study. The standard error of the regression coefficient can be interpreted as the variability of the beta coefficient over different samples (Kim & Kohout, 1975) and is used to test the significance of the beta values. As such, it does not represent as good a measure of sales volatility as does the standard error of the *estimate* which is unrelated to the the sampling distribution.

In addition, the coefficient of determination (R-squared) of the regression of the logarithm of value of shipments was not deemed as an appropriate measure of volatility because it is dependent upon the magnitude of the relationship between the logarithm of sales and time.

In other words, the coefficient of determination of the regression includes a component of the beta coefficient (The value of R-squared and the beta coefficients are related). Since the beta coefficient of this regression is the measure of percentage sales growth, having it as part of the volatility measure would have been inappropriate. In short, the volatility measure should not be a function of the sales growth measure.

$$VOL_i = SE_{i,72\text{-}78} \, / \, (Ave_{\,t=72 \text{ to } 78} \, (\log Y_{it}))$$

Where:
  SE = Standard error of the estimate for the equation in Equation IV-2
  Y   = Industry value of shipments in year t
  t   = Year
  i   = Four-digit S.I.C. industry

SE was calculated according to the following formula

$$SE_{i,72\text{-}78} = (StdDev \, Y_{i,72\text{-}78}) \times (SqrRoot \, (1\text{-}r^2))$$

Where: r^2 = the correlation coefficient between value of shipments and time

EQUATION IV-6: CALCULATION OF SALES VOLATILITY

Research and development intensity (RD). Research and development intensity was measured as the ratio of company-financed industry research and development expenditures to sales, averaged for the years 1976 and 1977. Research and development intensity measures the current flow of resources devoted to the generation of innovation within an industry and is the most commonly used measure of innovative input (Cohen & Levin, 1989). Acs and Audretsch (1989), and Orr (1974) used the same ratio in their studies of entry. The data for this study was obtained from the FTC's Line of Business Reports. Scherer and Ross stated that "The FTC Line of Business reports for 1974 through 1977 are the only reliable source on R&D spending data dis-aggregated to the four digit level of detail" (1990: 615). The unit of this variable is the percentage of total sales spent on research and development. When either 1976 or 1977 values were not available, the single-year value was used for this measure instead of the average. When both 1976 and 1977 values were not available, 1974 and/or 1975 data was used.

$$RD_i = Ave((R_{i,76}), (R_{i,77}))$$

Where:

R = Company-financed R&D intensity as reported by the FTC

i = Four-digit S.I.C. industry

EQUATION IV-7: CALCULATION OF RESEARCH AND DEVELOPMENT INTENSITY

Entry Barriers

Entry barriers used in the study included advertising intensity, capacity utilization, capital requirements, and industry concentration.

Advertising intensity (ADV). Advertising expenditures were measured as the ratio of industry advertising expenses to sales, averaged for the years 1976 and 1977. Previous researchers using the industry advertising to sales ratio as a measure of advertising intensity in studies of entry include Orr (1974), Duetsch (1975), Macdonald (1986), Gorecki (1975), and Harris (1976). Similar to the approach used herein, Harris (1976) averaged advertising intensity over a number of years. The unit of this variable is the percentage of total sales spent on media advertising. The source of advertising data was the Federal Trade Commission's *Annual Line of Business Report* for 1976 and 1977. When either 1976 or 1977 values were not available, the single-year value was used for this measure instead of the average. When both 1976 and 1977 values were not available, 1974 and/or 1975 data was used.

$$ADV_i = Ave((A_{i,76}), (A_{i,77}))$$

Where:

A = Media advertising intensity as reported by the Federal Trade Commission i = Four-digit S.I.C. industry

EQUATION IV-8: CALCULATION OF ADVERTISING INTENSITY

    Excess capacity (EXCAP). Excess capacity was measured as 100 minus the percentage practical plant capacity utilization. The percentage of plant capacity utilization was averaged for the years 1976 and 1977 and obtained from the U.S. Department of Commerce's *Survey of Plant Capacity.* When either 1976 or 1977 values were not available, the single year value was used for this measure instead of the average. When both 1976 and 1977 values were not available, 1978 and/or 1979 data were used.

$$EXCAP_i = Ave((100\text{-}CU_{i,76}), (100\text{-}CU_{i,77}))$$

Where:
    CU = Percentage practical plant capacity utilization
    i   = four-digit S.I.C. industry

EQUATION IV-9: CALCULATION OF EXCESS CAPACITY

    Log of capital requirements (LOGCR). Capital requirements were measured as the logarithm of the value of total book value of assets in the beginning of 1977 divided by the number of industry establishments in 1976 multiplied by 1000. The logarithm was taken in order that the regression coefficient would reflect the impact of a change in the percentage capital requirement on new venture formations. In addition, this transformation follows the precedent of other studies of the relationship between capital requirements and entry (Khemani & Shapiro, 1986; Shapiro & Khemani, 1987). Data on total assets was available from the 1977 Census of Manufactures. Data on the total number of establishments in the industry was acquired from the USELM database. In order to put the unit of this variable in thousands of dollars per establishment, the original capital requirements data were multiplied by 1000. This measure used 1977 Census data and 1976 USELM data since the years of these reports do not correspond exactly.

$$LOGCR_i = Log(ASS_{i,bg77} / EST_{i,76} \times 1000)$$

Where:
    ASS = Total industry assets
    EST = Number of industry establishments
    i   = Four-digit S.I.C. industry

EQUATION IV-10: CALCULATION OF LOG OF CAPITAL REQUIREMENTS

Industry concentration (C4). Industry concentration was measured as the four-firm concentration ratio in 1977. C4 has been used as an indicator of concentration in numerous studies which have examined entry including those of Harrigan (1981), Acs and Audretsch (1989), Duetsch (1975), and Highfield and Smiley (1987). Concentration ratio data for 1977 are available from the Census of Manufactures and are reported as a percentage of industry sales.

Organizational Inertia

The organizational inertia variables include the weighted average age of firms in the industry, the average size of firms in the industry, and the extent of industry unionization.

Weighted average age of firms (WTDAGE). The average age of firms in the industry was calculated for 1978 as a weighted average where weighting was based on employment size of firms. The age values were weighted so that the average age was not biased by the presence of young firms which accounted for a small percentage of industry output. Thus, the contribution of each firm's age to the average age variable was based on the sales contribution of that firm to the industry. Firms were classified in an industry according to their primary S.I.C. The calculation is described in Equation IV-11. The USEEM file provided the necessary data for this measure. The unit of this variable is years.

$$\text{WTDAGE}_{i,78} = (\sum_{j=1 \text{ to } n} (A_{ij,78} * \text{EMP}_{ij,78})) / T_{i,78}$$

Where:

i	= Four digit S.I.C. industry
j	= Firms
n	= Total number of firms in industry i
A_{ij}	= Age of firm j in industry i
EMP_{ij}	= Employment size of firm j in industry i
T_i	= Total industry employment = $\sum_{j=1 \text{ to } n} (E_{ij,78})$

EQUATION IV-11: CALCULATION OF WEIGHTED AVERAGE AGE OF FIRMS

Average size of firms (SZ). The average size of firms in the industry was based upon the employment of firms classified in the industry according to their primary four-digit S.I.C. The variable was calculated as the total employment of firms classified to be in the industry, divided by the total number of firms classified in the industry. The data for this variable was obtained from the USEEM file and was measured for 1978. The unit of this variable is number of employees.

$$SZ_i = \text{EMP}_{i,78} / \text{FIRMS}_{i,78}$$

Where:

EMP = Total firm employment
EST = Number of industry firms
i   = Four-digit S.I.C. industry
Firms are classified in the industry according to their *primary* four-digit S.I.C.

EQUATION IV-12 : CALCULATION OF AVERAGE SIZE OF FIRMS

Extent of unionization (UNION). The extent of unionization was measured as the percentage of all industry workers that belong to a union. This data is available from Freeman and Medhoff (1979a) and is based on Bureau of Labor Statistics data for the years 1968, 1970, and 1972. Unfortunately, data for years closer to the base year of the present study were not available. As a result, the unionization measure may not reflect declines in the extent of U.S. unionization which have been occurring in the last two decades. However, Acs and Audretsch (1989) used this measure in their more recent (in terms of base year of the study) investigation of small-firm entry in manufacturing, and it has been a valuable resource for research on labor relations (Kokkelenberg & Sockell, 1985). The Freeman & Medhoff data is reported by three-digit S.I.C. Consequently, the three-digit values were assigned to all of the four-digit industries within the pertinent three-digit categorization. In addition, the Freeman and Medhoff data utilized 1967 S.I.C. categorizations which are not directly comparable to the 1977 categorizations used in this study. Using the S.I.C. manual, translations from the 1967 to the 1977 categorization were performed, making the unionization data compatible with the rest of the database.

CHAPTER SUMMARY

This chapter explained the methodology and research design used to test the model of new venture formations. Multiple linear regression was utilized to examine the validity of the proposed hypotheses on a large sample of four-digit S.I.C. manufacturing industries. The analysis used a unique collection of secondary data sources, including the Small Business Administration's U.S. Establishment and Enterprise Longitudinal Microdata file, the Department of Commerce's *Census* and *Annual Survey of Manufactures*, the Federal Trade Commissions' *Annual Line of Business Data*, and others. New venture formations were measured as the logarithm of the number of new, independent establishments appearing in the industry over the four-year period from 1976 to 1980. The form of the regression model is predominantly semi-logarithmic, allowing interpretation of the relationships as the percentage effect of each independent variable on the percentage increase in new venture formations. Eleven independent variables are in the regression model. Specific industry dynamism variables include sales growth, niche dynamism, sales volatility, and research and development intensity. Entry barriers in the empirical model are advertising intensity, excess capacity, the logarithm of capital requirements, and four-firm industry concentration. Measures of organizational inertia include the weighted average age of firms, the average size of firms, and extent of unionization.   Specific calculations of each of these independent variables were described.

V

RESULTS

Chapter Overview

      This chapter presents the results of the data analysis performed relative to the proposed model of new venture formation in manufacturing industries. The purpose of this chapter is not to introduce implications, but to present the results without interpretation. The chapter begins with an examination of the descriptive statistics for each of the variables in the study. Then, the various bivariate relationships are presented and discussed. Next, the regression results and hypothesis tests are provided. Finally, the validity of the regression assumptions are examined. A discussion of the results is presented in the following chapter.

DESCRIPTIVE STATISTICS

New Venture Formations

      Descriptive statistics and a histogram on the number of venture formations are given in Figure V-1. The average number of new venture formations in the 382 industries over the four-year period of the study was 235.6, while the median level was much lower, at 88 formations. The standard deviation of this variable was 511.7, and the values ranged from 0 to 7037. The median is much lower than the average because the frequency distribution of new venture creations is highly positively skewed. The histogram indicates that most industries exhibit low levels of new venture formations, but that some industries

TABLE V-1: DESCRIPTIVE STATISTICS
(n=382)

Variable	Mean	Std Dev	Median	Min	Max
Entry					
# of Venture Formations (NVF)	235.634	511.662	88.000	0.000	7037.000
Log of New Venture Formations (LOGNVF)	1.924	0.661	1.945	-1.000	3.847
Dynamism					
Percent Sales Growth (PCTGRTH)	4.225	1.995	4.367	-5.478	12.148
Niche Dynamism (NICHEDYN)	3.245	4.718	1.612	0.000	41.793
Sales Volatility (VOL)	0.013	0.008	0.010	0.001	0.054
R&D Intensity (RD)	1.082	1.190	0.600	0.000	8.700
Entry Barriers					
Advertising Intensity (ADV)	1.610	2.224	0.850	0.000	14.450
Excess Capacity (EXCAP)	26.217	9.806	26.000	-0.500	66.000
Capital Requirements (CR)	2496.596	5143.813	765.453	23.988	41190.730
Log of Capital Requirements (LOGCR)	2.929	0.616	2.884	1.380	4.615
Four-Firm Concentration Ratio (C4)	37.654	19.890	35.000	4.000	93.000
Organizational Inertia					
Weighted Average Firm Age (WTDAGE)	39.270	19.287	34.205	9.210	122.930
Average Firm Size (SZ)	201.645	414.352	74.753	5.059	4240.086
Extent of Unionization (UNION)	45.597	17.368	47.000	0.000	90.000

Fig. V-1: Descriptive Statistics and Histogram For NVF

A. Descriptive Statistics

Mean	235.634	Median	88.000	Std dev	511.662
Kurtosis	89.414	Skewness	7.923	Minimum	.000
Maximum	7037.000				

B. Histogram
(Each star indicates approximately 4 cases)
(Interval Width = 50)

Count	Midpoint	
133	25	*********************************
77	75	*******************
34	125	*********
26	175	*******
16	225	****
17	275	****
14	325	****
8	375	**
5	425	*
7	475	**
5	525	*
3	575	*
3	625	*
7	675	**
2	725	*
2	775	*
1	825	
4	875	*
2	925	*
16	Extremes (>950)	****

have relatively high levels of formations.   Table V-2 shows the industries with the ten largest and ten smallest number of new venture formations.

For a number of reasons (which were also discussed in Chapter IV), NVF was transformed using the base 10 logarithm. The primary justification was that the transformation created a semi-logarithmic form of the regression model and thereby allowed interpretation of the effect of percentage change in the independent variables on the percentage change in new venture formations. In addition, the logarithmic transformation eliminated the skew in the NVF

TABLE V-2: HIGHEST AND LOWEST LEVELS OF NEW VENTURE FORMATION

A. Largest

S.I.C	Industry	NVF
2752	Commercial Lithographic Printing	7037
2751	Commercial Letterpress Printing	3539
3079	Miscellaneous Plastic Products	3299
3544	Special Dies, Tools, Jigs, & Fixtures	1925
2434	Wood Kitchen Cabinets	1753
2721	Periodicals	1399
2411	Logging Products and Contract Logging	1374
2731	Book Publishing	1353
3911	Precious Metal Jewelry	1326
2711	Newspapers	1325
2791	Typesetting	1273

B. Smallest

S.I.C.	Industry	NVF
2067	Chewing Gum and Chewing Gum Base	0
2296	Tire Cord and Tire Fabrics	1
3333	Primary Zinc Smelting	1
3761	Guided Missiles and Space Vehicles	1
3795	Tanks and Tank Components	1
3764	Space Propulsion Units and Parts	2
2044	Milled Rice and Byproducts	3
2063	Refined Beet Sugar and Byproducts	3
2074	Cottonseed Oil Mill Products	3
3331	Primary Copper Smelting	3

variable (See Figure V-1). The logarithmic transformation is a commonly recommended procedure for normalizing highly positively skewed variables. Lastly, many of the relationships between NVF and the independent variables were non-linear. Transformation of NVF eliminated much of the non-linearity between the dependent and independent variables. The specific nature of the non-linearity will be discussed in subsequent sections. Figure V-2 below shows the descriptive statistics and histogram for LOGNVF. The frequency distribution of LOGNVF is very close to a normal distribution, and a number of extreme values were brought in by the transformation.

Independent Variables

The average value of sales growth (PCTGRTH) was 4.2 percent and the standard deviation was 2 percent. Values ranged from -5.5 percent to 12.1 percent. The distribution of scores was close to normal.

The niche dynamism variable (NICHEDYN) was highly positively skewed. A number of factors accounted for the large skew in this variable. First, some industries had extremely high scores on this variable. Second, a large number of industries had only one product class, and were therefore assigned a value of zero for the NICHEDYN variable. Due to the skewness in this variable, the median (1.612 percent) probably best reflects the central tendency of the values. The values ranged from 0 to 41.8 percent, and the standard deviation was 4.7 percent. Despite the large skew of this variable, no transformation was performed. First, the variable is already in percentage terms such that transformation would have made interpretation of the relationship difficult. In addition, the skewness results primarily from the large numbers of cases which have a value of one for this variable. As a result, many transformations (i.e. logarithmic) would not have eliminated the skew anyway.

Values of sales volatility (VOL) ranged from .001 to .054, and averaged .013. The standard deviation was .009. The distribution was only slightly positively skewed.

Fig. V-2: Descriptive Statistics and Histogram for LOGNVF

A. Descriptive Statistics

Mean	1.924	Median	1.945	Std dev	.661
Kurtosis	.771	Skewness	-.341	Minimum	-1.000
Maximum	3.847				

B. Histogram
(Each star indicates approximately 4 cases)
(Interval Width = .5)

Count	Midpoint	
1	-.75	
0	-.25	
9	.25	**
16	.75	****
71	1.25	******************
113	1.7	****************************
97	2.25	************************
59	2.75	***************
13	3.25	***
3	3.75	*

The average level of company-financed research and development intensity (RD) for the 382 industries was 1.082 percent. Due to a number of high-end outliers, and a positively skewed distribution, the median (0.60 percent) was smaller than the mean value. The standard deviation of the values was 1.19 percent. Values ranged from a minimum of 0 to a maximum of 8.7 percent. Most industries spent relatively little on R&D, but a few spent a much larger percentage of their sales on R&D. Despite the skewness, the variable was not transformed because it was already in percentage terms.

The average and median values of this variable may seem lower than that typically reported for U.S. manufacturing industries. A number of reasons account for this dichotomy. First, the figures are only for company-financed R&D expenditures and therefore do not include R&D activities which are supported by the government. In addition, missing data acts to reduce the average R&D intensity values in the sample. As mentioned earlier, the sample is biased against highly concentrated industries. Comparison of sample to non-sample R&D values indicates (see Table IV-1) that the non-sample group had significantly higher average R&D intensity than the sample group (the non-sample average R&D intensity was 1.45 percent). However, even after this bias is taken into account, the R&D intensity reported by the FTC studies is still much lower than the 2 percent figure (for 1978) reported by National Science Foundation in its "Research & Development in Industry" publications. The lower values reported by the FTC may be due to the FTC's survey methodology, which collected R&D expenditures by line of business rather than by the primary S.I.C. of respondent firms.

Similar to research and development intensity, the distribution of advertising intensity (ADV) was positively skewed. Most industries spent relatively little on advertising (the median value was 0.85 percent), but some industries spent large amounts (up to 14.45 percent). The standard deviation of ADV was 2.22 percent. Again, no transformation was performed in order to maintain the percentage/ percentage interpretation of the results.

Percent excess capacity (EXCAP) closely approximated a normal distribution with an average value and median of 26 percent. The standard deviation was 9.8 percent, and the values ranged from -.5 percent (indicating that the industry was operating at greater than practical capacity), to 66 percent.

The average value of the log of capital requirements (LOGCR) was 2.93. The values ranged from 1.38 to 4.62, and the standard deviation was .616. The distribution of this variable was close to normal. Capital requirements were logarithmically transformed in order to allow interpretation of the regression coefficient as the effect of a percentage change in capital requirements on a percentage change in new venture formations. This follows the specification of other researchers (Khemani & Shapiro, 1986). The high skew of capital requirements (before taking the logarithm) further justifies the logarithmic transformation. The average value of capital requirements (before taking the logarithm) was $2,496,596 per establishment and the values ranged from $23,988 to $41,190,728.

The values of industry concentration (C4) ranged from 4 percent to a high of 93 percent, and averaged 37.6 percent. The standard deviation was 19.9 percent, and the distribution was fairly close to normal. As mentioned earlier, the sample was biased against highly concentrated industries due to missing data values. As a result the average industry concentration of the sample group was significantly lower than that of the non-sample group (the non-sample average industry concentration was 48.3 percent).

The distribution of weighted average age of firms (WTDAGE) ranged from 9.2 years to 122.9 years, and was slightly positively skewed. The mean weighted average age was 39.2 years, and the median was 34.2 years. The standard deviation was 19.3 years.

The average firm size variable (SZ) was somewhat positively skewed. Most industries had an average number of employees of less than 150, but a few industries were much larger. Values ranged from a low of 5.1 to a high of 4240.1 employees. The median value for SZ was 74.7 employees, and the standard deviation was 414.4 employees.

The average value of unionization (UNION) was 45.6 percent, and the standard deviation was 17.4 percent. The values ranged from 0 percent to 90 percent, and the distribution was close to normal.

BIVARIATE RELATIONSHIPS

Scatterplots

Figures V-3 to V-13 below show bivariate scatterplots between the independent variables and both the number of venture formations (NVF) and the log of the number of venture formations (LOGNVF). Bivariate linear regression equations are provided with each of the scatterplots.

It is evident from examination of these figures that the LOGNVF bi-variate relationships are stronger than the NVF bivariate relationships. For all of the independent variables except for EXCAP and WTDAGE, the R-squared for the bivariate relationship is higher when regressed with LOGNVF versus NVF. It is also apparent that many of the relationships between the independent variables and NVF are not linear. Consider, for example, Figures V-9 and V-10, which show the bivariate relations of NVF with LOGCR and C4 respectively. Visual examination of the scatterplots reveals a definite non-linearity in the relationship. In addition, the R-squared for the NVF/C4 relationship is only 0.122, while the R-squared for the LOGNVF/C4 relationship is 0.394. Similarly, the R-squared for the NVF/LOGCR relationship is only 0.088, while the R-squared for the LOGNVF/LOGCR relationship is 0.303. In short, the bivariate relationships support the use of LOGNVF instead of NVF as the dependent variable in the regression.

While the bivariate relationships do not provide a test of the various proposed hypotheses, it is interesting to note the direction of

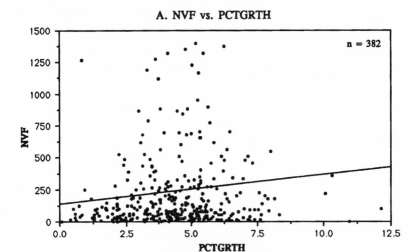

A. NVF vs. PCTGRTH

n = 382

* Some outlying datapoints are not shown
** Line Indicates Bivariate Least Squares Regression
y = 140.48 + 22.522x   R^2 = 0.008

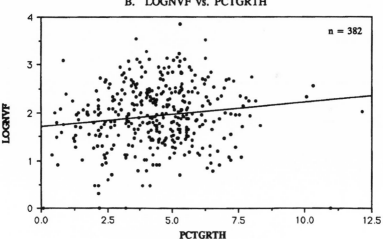

B. LOGNVF vs. PCTGRTH

n = 382

* Some outlying datapoints are not shown
** Line Indicates Bivariate Least Squares Regression
y = 1.7111 + 4.9975e-2x   R^2 = 0.023

Fig. V-3: PCTGRTH Scatterplots

A. NVF vs. NICHEDYN

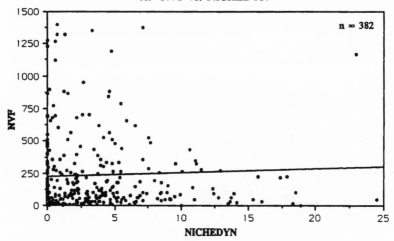

* Some outlying datapoints are not shown
** Line Indicates Bivariate Least Squares Regression
y = 226.03 + 2.9584x   R^2 = 0.001

B. LOGNVF vs. NICHEDYN

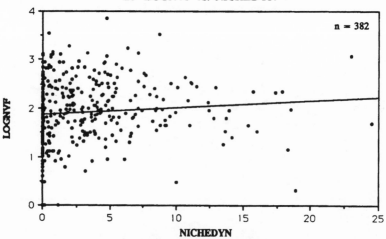

* Some outlying datapoints are not shown
** Line Indicates Bivariate Least Squares Regression
y = 1.8786 + 1.3441e-2x   R^2 = 0.009

Fig. V-4: NICHEDYN Scatterplots

A. NVF vs. VOL

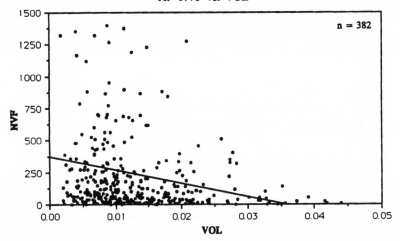

* Some outlying datapoints are not shown
** Line Indicates Bivariate Least Squares Regression
$y = 367.37 - 1.0350e+4x$ $R^2 = 0.026$

B. LOGNVF vs. VOL

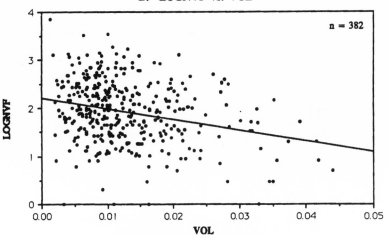

* Some outlying datapoints are not shown
** Line Indicates Bivariate Least Squares Regression
$y = 2.2099 - 22.602x$ $R^2 = 0.074$

Fig. V-5: VOL Scatterplots

A. NVF vs. RD

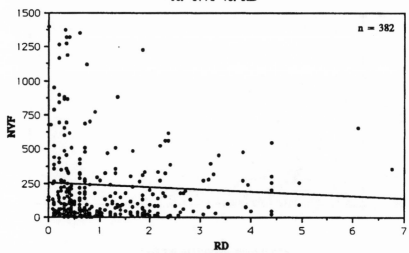

* Some outlying datapoints are not shown
** Line Indicates Bivariate Least Squares Regression
$y = 252.36 - 15.456x$ $R^2 = 0.001$

B. LOGNVF vs. RD

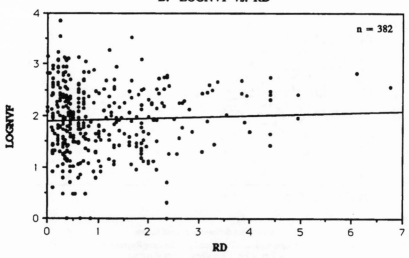

* Some outlying datapoints are not shown
** Line Indicates Bivariate Least Squares Regression
$y = 1.8918 + 2.8130e\text{-}2x$ $R^2 = 0.003$

Fig. V-6: RD Scatterplots

A. NVF vs. ADV

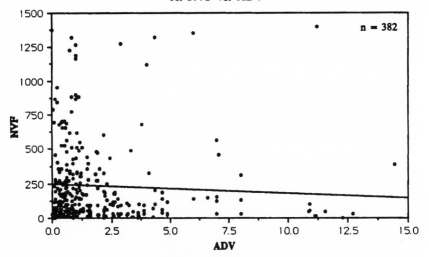

* Some outlying datapoints are not shown
** Line Indicates Bivariate Least Squares Regression
y = 246.16 - 6.5380x   R^2 = 0.001

B. LOGNVF vs. ADV

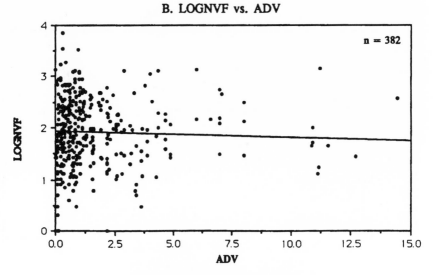

* Some outlying datapoints are not shown
** Line Indicates Bivariate Least Squares Regression
y = 1.9427 - 1.2724e-2x   R^2 = 0.002

Fig. V-7: ADV Scatterplots

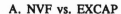

A. NVF vs. EXCAP

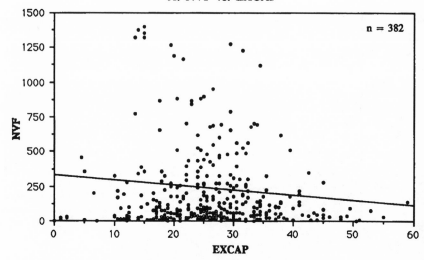

* Some outlying datapoints are not shown
** Line Indicates Bivariate Least Squares Regression
$y = 328.92 - 3.5581x$ $R^2 = 0.005$

B. LOGNVF vs. EXCAP

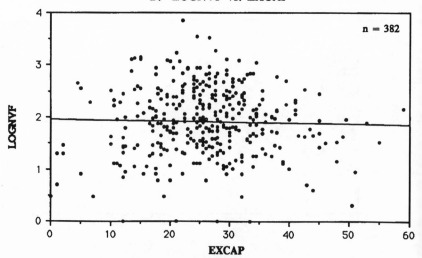

* Some outlying datapoints are not shown
** Line Indicates Bivariate Least Squares Regression
$y = 1.9670 - 1.7099e\text{-}3x$ $R^2 = 0.001$

Fig. V-8: EXCAP Scatterplots

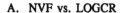

A. NVF vs. LOGCR

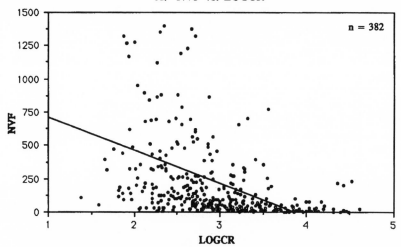

* Some outlying datapoints are not shown
** Line Indicates Bivariate Least Squares Regression
y = 957.36 - 246.37x   R^2 = 0.088

B. LOGNVF vs. LOGCR

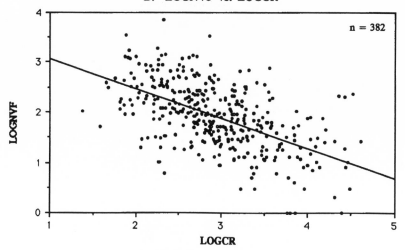

* Some outlying datapoints are not shown
** Line Indicates Bivariate Least Squares Regression
y = 3.6590 - 0.59289x   R^2 = 0.303

Fig. V-9: LOGCR Scatterplots

A. NVF vs. C4

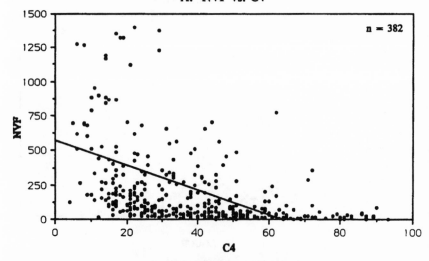

* Some outlying datapoints are not shown
** Line Indicates Bivariate Least Squares Regression
y = 574.31 - 8.9943x   R^2 = 0.122

B. LOGNVF vs. C4

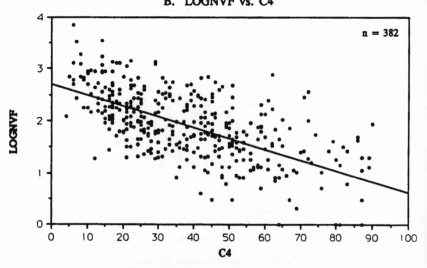

* Some outlying datapoints are not shown
** Line Indicates Bivariate Least Squares Regression
y = 2.7101 - 2.0925e-2x   R^2 = 0.394

Fig. V-10: C4 Scatterplots

A. NVF vs. WTDAGE

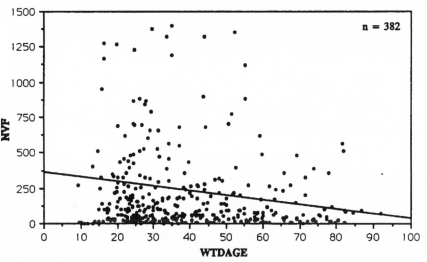

* Some outlying datapoints are not shown
** Line Indicates Bivariate Least Squares Regression
$$y = 361.56 - 3.2067x \quad R^2 = 0.015$$

B. LOGNVF vs. WTDAGE

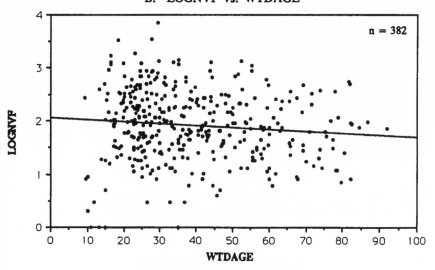

* Some outlying datapoints are not shown
** Line Indicates Bivariate Least Squares Regression
$$y = 2.0631 - 3.5866e\text{-}3x \quad R^2 = 0.011$$

Fig. V-11: WTDAGE Scatterplots

A. NVF vs. SZ

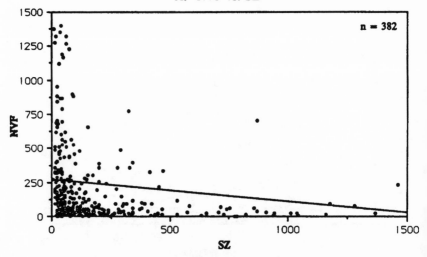

* Some outlying datapoints are not shown
** Line Indicates Bivariate Least Squares Regression
$y = 267.28 - 0.15695x$ $R^2 = 0.016$

B. LOGNVF vs. SZ

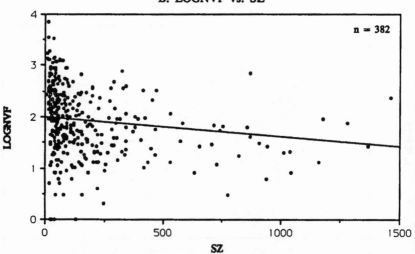

* Some outlying datapoints are not shown
** Line Indicates Bivariate Least Squares Regression
$y = 1.9989 - 3.8014e-4x$ $R^2 = 0.056$

Fig. V-12: SZ Scatterplots

A. NVF vs. UNION

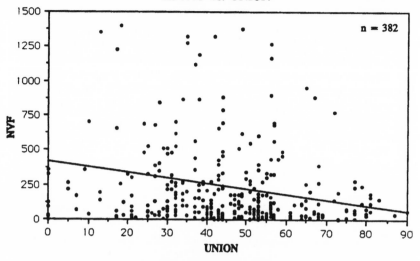

* Some outlying datapoints are not shown
** Line Indicates Bivariate Least Squares Regression
y = 414.54 - 3.9236x   R^2 = 0.018

B. LOGNVF vs. UNION

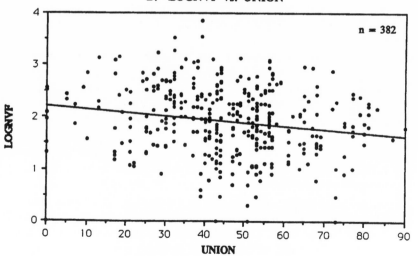

* Some outlying datapoints are not shown
** Line Indicates Bivariate Least Squares Regression
y = 2.2118 - 6.3504e-3x   R^2 = 0.028

Fig. V-13: UNION Scatterplots

each of the bivariate relationships in these figures. All of the relationships between LOGNVF and the dynamism variables were in the hypothesized positive direction except for sales volatility. As hypothesized, all of the entry barrier measures were negatively related to LOGNVF, but none of the inertia variables was in the hypothesized positive direction. Nonetheless, it is inappropriate to make conclusions from the bivariate relationships since the bivariate regressions do not account for the presence of the rest of the independent variables in the model. After presenting the correlations between the variables, the regression results and hypothesis tests will be described.

Correlations

Table V-3 below presents the correlations between the dependent and independent variables used in the regression analysis. The table also shows the two-tailed significance of each of the correlations. As expected, the correlation between NVF and LOGNVF is high, and significant. Also, a number of the independent variables are highly correlated to LOGNVF. VOL, C4, LOGCR, UNION, WTDAGE, and SZ are all significantly, negatively correlated to LOGNVF. PCTGRTH is the only variable which has a significant, positive correlation with the dependent variable. The independent variables with the highest correlations with LOGNVF are C4 and LOGCR.

These two variables (C4 and LOGCR) are also highly correlated with each other as well as with a number of the other independent variables. C4 had significant correlations with RD, ADV, LOGCR, UNION, WTDAGE, and SZ. LOGCR was significantly correlated with PCTGRTH, RD, EXCAP, LOGCR, ADV, UNION, WTDAGE, and SZ. Both WTDAGE and SZ are also correlated with a large number of the other independent variables. The correlation between LOGCR and C4 is the highest correlation between the independent variables. This is to be expected, since industries with high capital requirements logically can be expected to have fewer firms. This relationship also accounts for the high value of the correlation between SZ and LOGCR and C4. Moreover, it appears that industries with larger firms tend to have a larger weighted average age. Overall, the correlation matrix suggests that the four variables, C4,

TABLE V-3: CORRELATION MATRIX
(N=382)

	NVF	LOG NVF	PCT GRTH	NICH DYN	VOL	RD	ADV	EX CAP	LOG CR	C4	WTD AGE	SZ	UNION
NVF	1.000	.601**	.088	.027	-.162**	-.036	-.028	-.068	-.297**	-.350**	-.121*	-.127*	-.133**
LOGNVF		1.000	.150**	.096	-.272**	.050	-.043	-.026	-.551**	-.628**	-.105*	-.238**	-.167**
PCTGRTH			1.000	.011	-.138**	.210**	-.037	-.139**	.216**	-.008	.104*	.051	.092
NICHEDYN				1.000	.0005	.058	-.066	.049	-.0002	-.063	-.081	-.059	-.010
VOL					1.000	-.162**	-.133**	-.016	-.062	.075	-.171**	-.074	-.028
RD						1.000	-.013	.126*	.191**	.270**	.170**	.120*	-.059
ADV							1.000	-.005	-.101*	.138**	.171**	.0008	-.168**
EXCAP								1.000	-.107*	-.017	-.135**	-.121*	.016
LOGCR									1.000	.586**	.309**	.466**	.232**
C4										1.000	.287**	.343**	.183**
WTDAGE											1.000	.424**	.077
SZ												1.000	.162**
UNION													1.000

* - Significance <= .05 (two-tailed)
** - Significance <= .01 (two-tailed)

LOGCR, WTDAGE, and SZ partially capture the same variance and overlap to some degree. However, the correlations are not so large as to suggest that the four variables are measuring the same construct. Another relatively high correlation exists between C4 and RD. It appears that more highly concentrated industries spend a greater percentage of their sales on research and development. Also, faster growing industries tend to spend a higher percentage of their sales on research and development.

REGRESSION RESULTS

Significance Levels

Any test of significance requires a decision regarding the level of risk in rejecting a null hypothesis. If one chooses a 0.1 significance level (alpha), there is a ten percent chance of making a type-one error and rejecting the null hypothesis when the null hypothesis is, in fact, true. In other words, some relationships will appear to be significant just by chance. The lower the significance level set, the less the chance of making a type-one error, but the harder it is to conclude that a relationship does exist. Probably the most traditional approach is to set alpha equal to .05, and risk a 5 percent chance of a type-one error. The present research will utilize the .05 level, but will consider relationships which are significant at the 0.1 level as marginally significant. In addition, the actual significance probability (p) will be reported so that researchers can make their own conclusions on whether or not the null hypothesis should be rejected. Relationships with significance probabilities less than or equal to .01 will be considered highly significant.

Predicted Variance and Regression Significance

Table V-4 below presents the results of regressing LOGNVF on the eleven independent variables. The coefficient of multiple determination (R-squared) of the regression is 0.588, and the adjusted R-squared is 0.576. Approximately 58 percent of the variance in new venture formation is explained by the regression equation. The F-statistic for the regression is significant below the .01 level

TABLE V-4: REGRESSION RESULTS

Independent Variable	Predicted Sign	Regression Coefficient	Standardized Regression Coefficient	t	Signif. of t (one-tail)	Alternative Hypothesis Supported?
Industry Dynamism						
Percent Sales Growth (PCTGRTH)	+	0.0515	.156	4.288***	.0000	yes
Niche Dynamism (NICHEDYN)	+	0.0089	.064	1.892**	.0296	yes
Sales Volatility (VOL)	+	-17.8631	-.216	-6.085	n/a	no
R&D Intensity (RD)	+	0.0927	.167	4.456***	.0000	yes
Entry Barriers						
Advertising Intensity (ADV)	-	-0.0174	-.059	-1.605*	.0546	marginal
Excess Capacity (EXCAP)	-	-0.0049	-.072	-2.075**	.0194	yes
Log of Capital Requirements (LOGCR)	-	-0.4578	-.427	-8.995***	.0000	yes
Four-Firm Concentration Ratio (C4)	-	-0.0139	-.419	-9.057***	.0000	yes
Organizational Inertia						
Weighted Average Firm Age (WTDAGE)	+	0.0020	.057	1.474*	.0707	marginal
Average Firm Size (SZ)	+	0.000055	.034	0.849	.1983	no
Extent of Unionization (UNION)	+	-0.00075	-.020	-0.553	.2904	no

$R^2 = .588$

Adjusted $R^2 = .576$ F = 48.022***

N = 382   Significance of F = .0000

* - Significance <= .1 (one-tailed)
** - Significance <= .05 (one-tailed)
*** - Significance <= .01 (one-tailed)

(p=.0000), indicating that a relationship does exist between the independent and dependent variables.

Specific regression coefficients, and significance thereof, are discussed below. Regression coefficients can be interpreted as the change in the mean response of log of new venture formations for each unit change in the independent variable, given all the other independent variables are in the model and are held constant. Also, since the NVF has been logarithmically transformed, regression coefficients can be interpreted as the effect of a unit change in the independent variable on the percentage change in new venture formations.

Industry Dynamism

Hypotheses H1 through H4 proposed a positive relationship between new venture formations, and industry growth, niche dynamism, industry volatility, and research & development intensity. Table V-4 shows that three out of the four industry dynamism *null* hypotheses were rejected. PCTGRTH, NICHEDYN, and RD were all positively related to the log of the number of new venture formations. Contrary to the hypothesis H3, VOL was not positively related to LOGNVF.

Hypothesis H1 proposed a positive relationship between industry sales growth and new venture formation. As shown in Table V-4, the regression coefficient for PCTGRTH was 0.0515. Since this parameter is both positive and highly significant (p=.0000), we must reject the null hypothesis and conclude that there is a positive relationship between PCTGRTH and LOGNVF. The standardized regression coefficient for PCTGRTH was 0.156. This is one of the larger betas, indicating that this relationship is relatively strong.

Hypothesis H2 suggested a positive relationship between niche dynamism and new venture formation. The null hypothesis relative to niche dynamism is rejected at the 0.05 level. A positive, significant regression parameter (b=.0089, p=.03) was found between NICHEDYN and LOGNVF. Thus, it was concluded that there is a positive relationship between niche dynamism and new venture formation. The standardized regression coefficient was 0.064, indicating that although the hypothesis was supported, NICHEDYN was not one of the stronger predictors in the regression equation.

Hypothesis H3 suggested that a positive relationship exists between industry sales volatility and new venture formation. The regression coefficient for sales volatility was -17.86. Since the coefficient was negative, we cannot reject the null hypothesis with the one-tailed test. In this sample, there is no positive relationship between sales volatility and new venture formation. On the contrary, the regression coefficient indicated that a negative relationship may exist. In fact, if a two-tailed significance test had been performed, the VOL regression parameter would have been highly significant in the negative direction. This negative relationship was quite strong, as evidenced by the large standardized regression coefficient (beta = -0.216).

Hypothesis H4 proposed a positive relationship between research and development intensity and new venture formation. The research and development intensity regression parameter was both positive (b=.0927) and highly significant (p=.0000). Thus we reject the null hypothesis that there is no relationship between research and development intensity and new venture formation. We conclude that there is a positive relationship between RD and LOGNVF. The standardized regression coefficient was 0.167, indicating that this relationship is strong relative to some of the other variables.

Entry Barriers

Three of the four entry barrier *null* hypotheses were rejected by the analysis of the sample of manufacturing industries. In addition, the fourth null hypothesis was marginally rejected. Both the four-firm concentration ratio and the log of capital requirements were strongly related to the log of the number of new venture creations. Excess capacity did not have as strong an effect on new venture formations, but was significant. The negative coefficient of advertising intensity on new venture formations was only marginally significant.

Hypothesis H5 proposed a negative relationship between industry advertising intensity and new venture formation. The regression coefficient of advertising intensity was significant at the .1 level, but not at the .05 level (p=.0546). According to the criteria established earlier, hypothesis $H5_0$ can be only marginally rejected. Thus, it is likely that a relationship exists between advertising intensity and new venture formation, but it cannot be solidly concluded to exist. In addition, the strength of the relationship relative to the other variables is not great (beta=-.059).

Hypothesis H6 proposed a negative relationship between excess capacity and new venture formation. The regression coefficient between EXCAP and LOGNVF was -0.0049, and was significant at the .05 level (p=0.0194). Thus, the null hypothesis relative to excess capacity was rejected, and it was concluded that the existence of excess capacity in an industry is negatively related to new venture formation. The standardized regression parameter for this relationship is -0.072, indicating that the relationship is not one of the stronger ones in the model.

Hypothesis H7 argued that industry capital requirements are negatively related to new venture formation. The log of capital requirements regression parameter was both negative (b=-0.4578) and highly significant (p=.0000). Thus we reject the null hypothesis that there is no relationship between industry capital requirements and new venture formation. It is concluded that a negative relationship exists between capital requirements and new venture formation. In addition, the standardized regression coefficient for this variable was the largest parameter in the equation (beta=-0.427), indicating a very strong relationship.

Hypothesis H8 argued that industry concentration would exhibit a negative relationship with new venture formation. Since the C4 regression coefficient was negative and highly significant (b=-0.0139, p=.0000), $H8_0$ is rejected. The industry four-firm concentration ratio is negatively related to new venture creation. In addition, the standardized regression coefficient was one of the largest (beta=-0.419), indicating a strong relationship between industry concentration and new venture formation.

Organizational Inertia

Overall, the organizational inertia hypotheses were not sustained by the data. Two of the organizational inertia hypotheses were not supported. The third was only marginally significant. No relationship was found between the extent of unionization and the average size of firms and new venture formation. A marginally significant relationship was shown between the weighted average age of firms and new venture formation.

Hypothesis H9 argued that a positive relationship exists between the weighted average age of firms in the industry and new venture formation. The regression coefficient of WTDAGE was significant at the 0.1 level, but not at the .05 level (p=.0707). Thus, according to the criteria established earlier, the null hypothesis $H9_0$ can be only marginally rejected. It is likely that a relationship exists between the weighted average age of firms and new venture formation, but it cannot be solidly concluded to exist. In addition, the strength of the relationship relative to the other variables is not great (beta=-0.057).

Hypothesis H10 proposed a positive relationship between the average size of firms and new venture formation. The regression coefficient for SZ was not significant and the null hypothesis $H10_0$ cannot be rejected. There was no relationship between the average size of firms and new venture formation.

Hypothesis H11 proposed a positive relationship between the extent of unionization and new venture formation. The regression coefficient for unionization was -0.00075. Since the coefficient was negative and insignificant (p=.2904), we cannot reject the null hypothesis. In this sample, there was no positive relationship between average firm size and new venture formation.

VALIDITY OF REGRESSION ASSUMPTIONS

When performing regression analysis it is important to examine the validity of assumptions associated with this methodology. Issues relative to linearity, the properties of residuals, outliers, multicollinearity, and variable normality are discussed below.

Linearity of the Regression Function

The first issue is whether or not a *linear* regression function is appropriate to the model and data. The linearity of the regression can be evaluated through the use of variable scatterplots and residual plots. A number of these graphical examinations are discussed below.

First of all, bivariate scatterplots can be examined to see if a non-linear relationship is evident (Norusis, 1990). While a bivariate relationship does not always imply that a similar relationship exists in a multivariate model, bivariate plots provide a useful starting point for evaluating the linearity of a multivariate model. The bivariate scatterplots presented above in Figure V-3 through V-13 reveal that linear relationships appear to exist between the logarithm of new venture formation and the independent variables.

A second methodology of evaluating the linearity of a regression function is to examine residual scatterplots. A plot of the predicted value of the dependent variable versus the residuals is a useful means to examine the linearity of the overall regression function (Norusis, 1990). Figure V-14 below shows the standardized predicted value of the log of new venture creation versus the standardized regression residuals. If a linear relationship exists, the residuals are expected to be randomly distributed about a horizontal line through zero.   Visual examination of this plot reveals that the linearity assumption has been met. It is interesting to note that the same residual plot for the regression without logarithmic transformation of NVF reveals that the linearity assumption would not have been met if NVF were used as the dependent variable in the regression. This provides further evidence to support the use of LOGNVF instead of NVF as the measure of new venture formation.   It appears that a semi-log relationship is more appropriate for most variables in predicting new venture formations.

Fig. V-14: Standardized Predicted
Values vs. Standardized Residuals

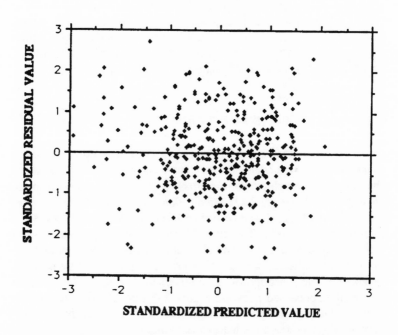

Plots of residuals against the independent variables can also be used to examine the validity of the linearity assumption (Norusis, 1990).   Examination of the residual plots for each of the eleven independent variables suggest that no non-linear relationships exist.

In summary, the bivariate scatterplots and the residual graphs do not indicate the existence of non-linearity in the regression equation. As a result, the model and associated data are concluded to meet the assumption of linearity of the regression function.

Properties of Residuals

Multiple linear regression also requires the validity of a number of assumptions relative to the residual values (otherwise known as error terms) (Norusis, 1990; Neter, Wasserman, & Kutner, 1983). The first assumption here is that the residuals are independent. The second is that the residuals are normally distributed, and the third is that the errors have constant variance. The validity of these properties in the regression model are discussed below.

Residual independence (Serial Correlation). Problems with non-independent errors usually occur only when time series data are collected (Neter, et. al., 1983). Since this study is not a time series study, the potential for non-independent errors is minimal. In addition, when the sample size is large, the validity of this assumption can be ignored for practical purposes (Neter, et. al., 1983). Since the present sample is rather large, non-independence of errors, even if it did exist, is not problematic.

Residual normality. Residuals in a regression model are also assumed to be normally distributed (Neter, et. al., 1983). One method of examining the assumption of normality is to plot a frequency distribution thereof (Norusis, 1990). A histogram of the present regression residuals is shown in figure V-15. In Figure V-15, the asterisks (*) indicate the frequency of cases for each interval value of the residuals. The colons (:) indicate the frequency that would be expected if the distribution of residuals were normal. Visual examination of the histogram reveals that the distribution of residuals is not perfectly normally distributed, but it is relatively close. Since an exact normal distribution is not expected (Norusis, 1990), Figure V-15 appears to validate the assumption that the errors are normally distributed.

An additional means to validate the normality of errors assumption is to examine a normal probability plot. A normal probability plot graphs the cumulative distribution of residuals against

Fig. V-15: Histogram of Standardized
Regression Residual

```
N      Exp N                    (* = 1 Case,  : = Normal Curve)
1      .29      Out *
0      .59      3.00:
1      1.49     2.67 :
1      3.41     2.33 *   :
12     6.97     2.00 ******:*****
10     12.77    1.67 **********   :
25     20.96    1.33 ******************:****
28     30.81    1.00 ***************************   :
33     40.57     .67 ****************************   :
43     47.86     .33 *************************************   :
63     50.56     .00 **********************************************:************
48     47.86    -.33 *************************************.
51     40.57    -.67 ***********************************:**********
25     30.81    -1.00 ***********************   :
21     20.96    -1.33 ******************:
10     12.77    -1.67 *********   :
1      6.97     -2.00 *      :
7      3.41     -2.33 **:****
1      1.49     -2.67 :
0      .59      -3.00:
1      .29      Out *
```

what would be expected under conditions of normality (Norusis, 1990).
Figure V-16 shows the normal probability plot for the present sample.
In the figure, the asterisks (*) represent the cumulative distribution of
residuals, and the periods represent the distribution expected under
conditions of normality. Since the asterisks depart only slightly from
the expected distribution, the assumption of normality again seems to
be verified.

　　　　A final methodology for determining normality is to perform
an actual statistical test to determine if the errors are normally
distributed. However, for large sample sizes (as is the present case),
such tests almost always reject the hypothesis that the distribution is
normal (Norusis, 1990). Consequently, these tests were not performed.

　　　　Based on the histogram of residuals and the normal probability
plot, it was concluded that the regression residuals are close to being
normally distributed and the assumption of normally distributed error
terms has been met.

　　　　Constant variance of error terms (homoscedasticity).
Problems of heteroscedasticity occur when the variance of the error
terms are not constant across all the values of the independent variables
(Norusis, 1990). Residual plots can be used to examine the validity of
this assumption.

Fig. V-16: Normal Probability Plot
Based on Standardized Residuals

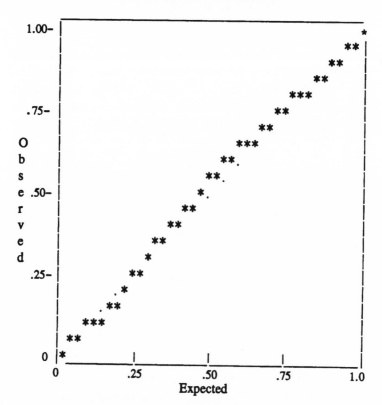

Plotting the residual values against the predicted values is one useful method of identifying whether heteroscedasticity exists (Neter, et al., 1983; Norusis, 1990). The residual/predicted scatterplot was given earlier in Figure V-14. Heteroscedasticity is indicated when the spread of the residuals varies across the range of predicted values (Norusis, 1990). Visual examination of Figure V-14 does not reveal the presence of any non-constancy in the error variances.

Residuals plotted against the independent variables is another means of examining whether the variance of errors is constant (Neter, et. al., 1983; Norusis, 1990). Again, heteroscedasticity exists if variation in the spread of residuals exists across the values of the independent variable (Norusis, 1990). Examination of the independent variable/residual plots reveals that a number of the residual plots have a trapezoidally shaped scatter. The plots with a trapezoidally shaped residual plot include VOL, RD, NICHEDYN, and SZ. At first glance, one might conclude that the trapezoidal shapes indicate heteroscedasticity of the errors. However, an additional factor needs to be considered before making this conclusion. All of the independent variables with trapezoidally shaped residual distributions are also positively skewed. As a result, values of the independent variable which are further from the mode have fewer frequencies, and the residual plots will tend to appear trapezoidal even if the error variance is constant. Thus, the trapezoidal shape in the plots of the aforementioned variables does not necessarily indicate the existence of heteroscedasticity. In fact, closer examination of each of the plots indicates that the spread of residuals would likely be even if the variables were normally distributed. In short, these plots provide evidence that the validity of the homoscedasticity assumption is met for most of the variables and likely met for the others.

In summary, the plot of residuals against the regression-predicted values supports the validation of the homoscedasticity assumption. Plots of residuals against the independent variables do not provide enough evidence to reject the conclusion of the residual/predicted values plot. It can safely be concluded that the error terms have constant variance.

Outliers

Another issue in the evaluation of a fitted regression model is the influence of extreme data points on the regression results. A case may be extreme relative to its independent or dependent variable value, or both (Neter, et. al., 1983). In addition, some outliers have a strong influence on the regression function, while others do not (Neter, et al., 1983). Thus, analysis of extreme cases requires consideration of both their outlying nature and the extent of their influence on the fitted function. Neter et al. (1983) suggest that independent and dependent variable outliers should be identified using leverage values and studentized deleted residuals, respectively. Then, the influence of each outlying case should be tested using Cook's D.

Use of the leverage values and studentized deleted residuals does not reveal any extreme outliers. More importantly, none of the outliers has a significant value for Cook's D. Thus, no outliers are influential in determining the fitted regression. As a result, it does not appear that the existence of outliers has a disproportionate effect on the resultant model. Outliers have not created any difficulties with fitting the dataset to the model.

Multicollinearity

A potentially serious problem with multiple regression models is the existence of multicollinearity. Multicollinearity occurs when there is a high correlation between the independent variables (Norusis, 1990). While multicollinearity does not affect the total explanatory power of the model (does not affect the R-squared value or the predicted value of the independent variable), it does have a number of serious effects. High correlations between the independent variables tend to make the regression coefficients unstable and therefore result in difficulties when making conclusions about the effect of specific independent variables on the dependent variable (Neter, et. al., 1983). For example, two highly correlated independent variables can result in small beta weights for both variables which mislead interpretation of their effect sizes. Correlations between the independent variables can also result in substantial variation in beta weights, depending on which variables are in the model. In addition, multicollinearity makes it harder to prove the significance of regression coefficients and thereby increases type II errors.

Numerous methods can be used to detect multicollinearity. Examination of bivariate correlation coefficients is probably the simplest methodology, but this methodology does not account for anything more than the collinearity between pairs of variables. A much more effective method is to examine variance inflation factors (VIF). Variance inflation factors measure how much the variance of the regression coefficients increase relative to when the independent variables are not related (Neter, et al., 1983). A VIF value for a given independent variable is equal to one when that variable is not linearly related to the other independent variables (Neter, et. al., 1983). Values greater than one indicate the presence of a linear relationship.

Neter et al. (1983) suggest a number of tests using VIF's to indicate the severity of multicollinearity. The first test is to examine the VIFs of specific independent variables. If the maximum value of the VIFs is greater than ten, considerable multicollinearity may exist. The highest variance inflation factors were for C4 and LOGCR (1.920 and 2.023 respectively). These two variables are highly correlated (r=.586), but the VIFs are not large enough to indicate any serious problem exists. A second test is examine the mean VIF value. A mean VIF value considerably larger than one indicates serious multicollinearity problems. The mean value of the VIFs for the present model is not much greater than one (1.345), again suggesting that multicollinearity is not a concern in the present model. In conclusion, the above tests indicate that multicollinearity is not a problem with the regression model.

Variable Normality

A number of the independent variables were positively skewed. While normally distributed variables are not required by least squares regression models, the inferential tests on individual regression coefficients require the use of t-tests. One of the assumptions of t-tests is that the variables are normally distributed (Glass & Hopkins, 1984). Thus, consideration was given to transforming some of the independent variables before applying the regression model to the data. However, this was not done for a number of reasons. First of all, t-tests are robust relative to the requirement for normally distributed variables (Glass & Hopkins, 1984). In other words, non-normal variables have little effect on the outcome of t-tests. In addition, the existing semi-logarithmic form of the model allows interpretation of most of the regression coefficients in percentage-percentage terms.

Conclusions on Regression Assumptions

Critical examination of the model and data indicates that the analysis meets the requirements of the linear regression methodology. First of all, any problems of non-linearity are solved by the logarithmic transformation of the dependent variable. Second, it appears that the residuals are independent, normally distributed, and homoscedastic. Third, outliers have not created any problems in the fitted regression function. Fourth, the presence of multicollinearity is minimal. Finally, the robustness of t-tests to non-normal variable distributions mitigates the potentially detrimental effect of a number of positively skewed independent variables. In sum, the assumptions of regression analysis have been met by the data and fitted model.

CHAPTER SUMMARY

Regression results indicate that the independent variables are highly predictive of new venture formations. The regression model explains 58 percent of the variance in new venture formations. Most of the industry dynamism variables have the hypothesized positive effect on new venture formations. Of the dynamism variables, R&D intensity and percentage sales growth are the strongest predictors of new venture formations, but niche dynamism also has a significant positive impact. Contrary to the hypothesis, sales volatility has a negative effect on new venture formations. Entry barriers are found to have strong negative effects on new venture formations, although the effect of advertising intensity is only marginally significant. Capital requirements and industry concentration are highly related to new venture formations. Excess capacity also has a significant negative relation. The organizational inertia measures, however, do not show the relationships expected. Both the extent of unionization and the average size of firms in the industry are not found to be related to new venture formations. The weighted average age of firms in the industry does have a positive effect but it is only marginally significant. Various analysis shows that the empirical model meets the assumptions of multiple linear regression analysis.

VI

DISCUSSION OF RESULTS, LIMITATIONS, AND FUTURE RESEARCH

Chapter Overview

This chapter provides a discussion of the results presented in Chapter V, describes a number of limitations which were inherent in the study, and suggests future research topics. The discussion of the results begins with a note on causality and then moves into interpretation of the empirical findings relative to each of the three conceptual variables: industry dynamics, entry barriers, and organizational inertia. Then, a number of general theoretical implications are discussed. Limitations concerning model specification, measures, data sources, and generalizability are then presented. The chapter ends with a number of suggestions for future research which might be used to extend and further test the theoretical model.

DISCUSSION OF RESULTS

A Note on Causality

Although the analysis was performed so that the measures of the independent variables were lagged relative to the measure of new venture formations, this lagging method is probably not sufficient to allow one to conclude that an independent variable/dependent variable causality exists between the variables. The establishment of causality requires the more rigorous conditions of an experimental design which was not possible to construct with the data available. As a result, strict interpretation of the results cannot imply a direction of causality. However, the discussion that follows often speaks in terms of cause and effect relationships. These causal implications are based on theoretical arguments which imply a given direction of effects.

New Venture Formations

Before moving to a discussion of the results of the regression model, it is interesting to note some of the descriptive findings on new venture formations. The average number of new ventures formed in the sample industries over the four-year period of the study was 235. However, the average was affected by the skewed distribution of this variable. The median number of new ventures started in the sample industries was 88, and over 200 (55%) of the industries had less than 100 new venture creations. Thus, most manufacturing industries have relatively few new ventures formations (about 20 to 25 per year). However, some industries are characterized by high levels of new venture formations, and a few are prolific in spawning new firms. The largest number of new ventures were formed in the commercial lithographic printing industry (7037 new ventures), and six of the ten with the largest numbers of formations were printing or publishing industries. Industries which registered the ten least number of venture formations were mostly military and space-oriented industries (guided missiles, tanks, and space propulsion), agricultural processing industries (milled rice, beet sugar refining, cottonseed oil mill products, and chewing gum and base), or ore processing industries (copper smelting and zinc smelting).

Total Variance Explained

The empirical model explained 58 percent of the variance in new venture formations in the sample. The strong explanatory power of the independent variables indicates that, overall, the model is a powerful predictor of new venture formations. In addition, the magnitude of the impact of independent variables is larger than that observed in most prior entry studies. For example, Acs and Audretsch (1989), Hamilton (1985), and Highfield and Smiley (1987), explained 18, 27, and 32 percent of the variance in entry, respectively. This may support Hamilton's (1985) conclusion that barriers to entry (particularly cost of entry barriers) have a stronger impact on independent firms than on dependent firms.

Specific Impacts of the Independent Variables

The proposed model implies that new venture formations are impacted by states of disequilibrium and the availability of opportunities in an industry, and that the availability of opportunities are a function of industry dynamics. In addition, the extent to which new ventures are able to exploit opportunities is a function of the constraints on existing firms and on firm formation. Entry barriers are argued to act as constraints on the exploitation of opportunities by new ventures. Organizational inertia is contended to constrain existing firms from exploiting opportunities, thereby leaving them open for new ventures.

Overall, the empirical analysis provides preliminary support for the model. As mentioned earlier, the independent variables explain a large percentage of the variance in new venture formations, and the relationships are mostly in the hypothesized direction. In general, industry dynamism has a positive impact on new venture formations, and entry barriers do constrain venture creations. However, the hypothesized effects of organizational inertia are not evident in the regression. Specific results relative to industry dynamics, entry barriers, and organizational inertia are presented below. Table VI-1 provides a summary of the results of the regression model. As the reader examines these results and moves through the discussion, he/she should keep in mind that the regression coefficient is indicative of the effect of the independent variable on new venture formations, given that all of the other independent variables are in the model. In other words, the regression coefficient represents the effect of each independent variable after the effects of the other independent variables has been partialled out.

Industry dynamism. The empirical analysis supports a link between industry dynamism and the creation of new ventures. Three of the four dynamism variables has the hypothesized positive relation with new venture formations. It appears that industry dynamics do create opportunities for exploitation by the formation of new ventures.

TABLE VI-1: SUMMARY OF RESULTS

Hypothesis	Finding	Significance
1	Industry sales growth increases the rate of new venture formations.	p=.000
2	The extent of niche sales dynamism encourages the formation of new ventures.	p=.030
3	Sales volatility acts as a barrier to the entry of new ventures and probably serves as an indicator of risk.	n/a
4	R&D intensity positively impacts the rate of new venture formations.	p=.000
5	Advertising intensity had a marginally significant, negative barrier effect on new venture formations. The negative barrier effect may have been mitigated by positive differentiation effects.	p=.055
6	The existence of excess capacity dissuades the formation of new ventures.	p=.019
7	Capital requirements act as a strong barrier to the establishment of new ventures.	p=.000
8	Industry concentration constrains the ability of new ventures to form.	p=.000
9	The weighted age of firms in an industry has a marginally positive impact on new venture formations.	p=.071
10	The age of firms in an industry has no effect on the rate of new venture formations.	p=.198
11	The extent of industry unionization has no effect on the rate of new venture formations.	p=.290

Sales growth. With a standardized regression coefficient of 0.156, the percentage annual industry sales growth has a relatively strong effect on the rate of new venture formations. The strong positive effect of industry sales growth is parallel to the findings of other studies of entry (MacDonald, 1986; Hamilton, 1985; Highfield & Smiley, 1987; Acs & Audretsch, 1989) and indicates that market growth creates important opportunities for new venture formation.

Research & development intensity. Research and development intensity also has a strong positive effect on new venture formations. The standardized regression coefficient for this variable is 0.167. This strong positive relation is counter to some arguments which view research and development expenditures as an additional capital requirement that deters entry (Acs & Audretsch, 1989). These results indicate that the positive opportunity-creating effect of research and development intensity is stronger than its capital requirement barrier effect for independent entrants in manufacturing industries. The importance of industry technological intensity as an opportunity creator is supported by studies which document spin-off entrepreneurs who leave existing firms to form high-technology companies (Mitton, 1989; Cooper, 1985). Such technological entrepreneurs may be overcoming technology barriers to entry by the knowledge they gain in previous positions and by the availability of venture capital (Florida & Kenney, 1988; Timmons & Bygrave, 1986).

Niche dynamism. Niche dynamism represents an innovative operationalization of the sales growth dynamics occurring within industry niches. Basically, niche dynamism measures the extent to which five-digit product classes within each industry are changing size (in terms of sales) in relation to one another. It is an important variable because it indicates when certain niches are growing, regardless of whether or not the industry as a whole is growing. Thus, the positive, significant coefficient (standardized coefficient=.064) reveals that the greater the temporal variability in sales shares of the niches, the greater the new venture formations. The implication of this result is that industry niche growth creates opportunities for new ventures to exploit. The fact that this variable is significant even with percent industry sales growth in the model indicates that the changes occurring in niches definitely play a role beyond that of industry sales growth. This finding parallels the theoretical propositions of strategic group theory, which argues that strategic groups parallel industry niches (Hatten & Hatten, 1987), and that specific niches can be targeted to help ease entry into an industry (Caves & Porter, 1977). Porter (1980) also views the targeting of new and growing niches as an effective strategy for industry entry. In sum, the positive relation between niche dynamism and new venture formation supports the contention that the sales dynamics of niches create opportunities for exploitation by new ventures.

Sales volatility. Contrary to the proposed hypothesis, sales volatility is not found to be positively related to new venture formations. In fact, sales volatility has a strong negative effect on new venture formations (standardized regression coefficient=-0.216). Sales volatility is used as a measure of industry dynamism because it has been proposed to be a measure of dynamism in the organization literature (i.e., Dess & Beard, 1984). However, the results bring into question this measure's validity as an indicator of dynamism *as conceptualized herein*. The meaning of dynamism in the present model focuses on its opportunity-creating aspects. In contrast, the sales volatility of an industry could equally destroy opportunities as often as it creates them. The reader may recall that the sales volatility measure was based upon the standard error of the estimate of the regression of industry sales over time and can be interpreted as the extent of dispersion of the sales data about the trend line. As such, this measure might be viewed more appropriately as a measure of risk and uncertainty than as a measure of dynamism as conceptualized herein. Similar measures of the variability in profit and sales have been used to portray the risk inherent in an industry and have been considered to be entry barriers (Winn, 1975; Highfield & Smiley, 1987; Harris, 1976; Orr, 1974).

In summary, sales volatility appears to be more a measure of the risk and uncertainty inherent in an industry than it is a measure of opportunity-creating dynamism. This finding has a number of important implications for future research. First of all, the conceptualization of dynamism as seen and measured by organization researchers has a risk component that needs to be recognized in future studies. Second, not all changes in industries have positive, opportunity-creating effects. Some changes do not create opportunities, and some may even destroy the number of opportunities available in an industry.

Moreover, the view of Knight (1921) and others who see a linkage between uncertainty, entrepreneurship, and profitability may need modification to address these findings. In short, uncertainty alone does not lead entrepreneurship and economic profit unless the uncertainty is associated with positive, opportunity-creating changes in industry environments.

Finally, these findings suggest that the view of dynamism as espoused herein more closely approximates organizational researchers' concept of "environmental munificence" than it does their concept of environmental dynamism. Environmental munificence represents the "extent to which the environment can support sustained growth", and has been argued to be a function of industry growth and profitability levels (Dess & Beard, 1984: 55). Perhaps organizational researchers should consider using the dynamism measures from this study (percent sales growth, niche dynamism, and research and development intensity) as measures of environmental munificence. In addition, organizational researchers could utilize the theory developed herein to predict the munificence of organizational environments based on industry dynamism and the existence of a state of disequilibrium.

Entry barriers. Entry barriers were found to be strongly negatively related to the creation of new ventures in manufacturing industries. In particular, capital requirements and industry concentration were highly negatively related to new venture formations. Excess capacity was also negatively related to the dependent variable, but advertising intensity was only marginally so $(0.05 < p < 0.1)$. In general the results support the prior industrial organization economics theory which contends that entry barriers constrain the ability of new ventures to enter industries.

Capital requirements. The large negative regression coefficient for the capital requirements measure (standardized coefficient=-0.427) indicates that capital requirements strongly limit the ability of new ventures to form. However, the exact value of this relationship is questionable because of some multicollinearity between capital requirements and industry concentration. Since these two variables are correlated, it is difficult to make firm conclusions regarding the relative impact of each on new venture formations. Nonetheless, the relationships are so strong that it is safe to conclude that both variables constrain new venture formations.

In summary, it appears that capital requirements strongly inhibit the formation of new ventures. The barrier effect of capital requirements has been verified in other studies of entry (Shapiro & Khemani, 1987; MacDonald, 1986, Hamilton, 1985; Orr, 1974). However, Hamilton's (1985) study is especially pertinent to the interpretation of these results. Hamilton found that capital requirements deterred the entry of independent firms, but not dependent firms. As a result, the strong capital requirement barrier effect evidenced in this study may not impact non-independent entrant firms. Theoretically, capital requirements should not have as large a barrier impact on dependent entrants since they may have access to the financial resources of their parent organizations.

Industry concentration. Industry Concentration also had a strong impact on rates of new venture formations. The standardized regression coefficient for industry concentration was the second largest in the regression (standardized coefficient=-0.419). However, as mentioned above, the exact value of the coefficient is questionable due to the multicollinearity between industry concentration and capital requirements.

Overall, this result may shed light on the argument about whether industry concentration really does act as an entry barrier. Some authors have argued that industry concentration does not act as a barrier to small-scale entry (Duetsch, 1975; Kunkel & Hofer, 1991). This contention is not supported by the present results nor by Hamilton, who also found a negative relation between concentration and independent entry. Independent ventures are likely to enter industries at a small scale rather than at a large scale. Therefore, the findings of this study are contrary to the arguments of Duetsch and Kunkel and Hofer, and indicate that small-scale entry is inhibited by a high level of industry concentration. Instead, the results support the traditional contention that industry concentration acts as a barrier to entry and new venture formations.

Excess capacity. The extent of excess capacity also was negatively related to new venture formations. The relation was moderately strong with a standardized regression coefficient of -0.072. The interpretation of this result is that higher excess capacity constrains the formation of new ventures. Theoretically, the barrier effect of excess capacity results from two possible mechanisms. First, the existence of excess capacity in an industry means that the entry of a large-scale venture will have a greater depressing impact on post-entry industry price and profitability levels (Scherer & Ross, 1990). Second, the existence of excess capacity may indicate that incumbents are using capacity levels as a means of strategic entry deterrence and therefore signalling their willingness to fight price wars (Dixit, 1982; Spence, 1977).

One might be led to conclude that the existence of excess capacity restricts new venture formation because it is also indicative of the lack of industry growth. In fact, the correlation between excess capacity and percent sales growth is significant and negative ($r=-.139$), supporting the expected inverse relationship between these two variables. However, given that sales growth is in the regression model, the proper interpretation of the negative excess capacity coefficient is that excess capacity has a barrier effect after the effect of sales growth has been partialled out.

Advertising intensity. The negative regression coefficient of advertising was only marginally significant ($0.05 < p < 0.1$). This puts into question whether advertising acts as a barrier to the formation of new ventures in manufacturing industries. The marginally significant negative coefficient is indicative that there may be some barrier effects, but the weak magnitude of the relationship suggests that advertising may have other impacts on new venture formations. Yip (1982) suggested that advertising has an entry-inducing effect, since it allows the pursuit of a greater variety of heterogeneous strategies. This alternate perspective fits well with some of the theory suggested relative to the niche dynamism variable. Arguments on niche dynamism suggest that the existence of niches and growing niches increases the opportunities available for potential new venture entrants. Since advertising intensity is an indicator of the extent of product differentiation, it may also be an indicator of the number of niches available in an industry. Higher advertising intensity may mean that there are more niches available for potential entrants to target and therefore, it has a positive effect on new venture formations. In fact, this positive effect could explain why some other empirical studies of entry have not found a negative impact of advertising on entry (Acs & Audretsch, 1989; Highfield & Smiley, 1987; MacDonald, 1986; Harrigan, 1981). Perhaps future studies of entry and new venture formations should reconsider the traditional viewpoint that advertising intensity serves as a barrier to entry and recognize its potential positive effects.

Organizational inertia. Of the three major conceptual variables in the study, the empirical results on organizational inertia were the only ones which did not support the proposed hypotheses. Two of the three inertia variables had no significant effect on new venture formations, and the other, weighted average age of firms, had only a marginally significant (0.05<p<0.1), positive effect. A number of possibilities could account for the poor showing of these variables in the regression equation. The most evident is that organizational inertia does not affect new venture formations. However, the alternative possibility is that the variables represent inappropriate measures of inertia. Given the innovative nature of the inertia operationalizations, this is entirely possible.

Inertia is operationalized with three measures: the weighted average age of firms in the industry, the average size of firms in the industry, and the extent of unionization. These measures are based on the assumptions that individual firm inertia is a function of its age, size, and unionization and that the industry level of inertia could be estimated by aggregating the characteristics of individual firms. This raises two fundamental questions. First, are age, size, and unionization of firms actually indicators of their level of inertia? And second, can we obtain an industry level measure of inertia by aggregating individual firm characteristics?

Relative to the first question, authors of a number of perspectives have suggested a relationship between firm age and size and inertia (See Chapter II). In fact, the theoretical bases for these relationships are quite strong. Empirical evidence is quite another matter. Although some authors have used organizational size as a measure of inertia (Keats & Hitt, 1988; Dean & Snell, 1991), neither organizational age nor size has been empirically shown to be related to inertia. Nor have any variables been examined which might moderate the age/inertia or size/inertia relationships. Clearly, further empirical research is necessary on the relationship between age and size and inertia. Similarly, a number of theoretical arguments and individual examples can be used to imply a unionization/inertia relationship, but no rigorous quantitative empirical research has directly tested this relationship.

The other important question was whether or not age, size, and unionization of individual firms can be aggregated to provide an industry level measure of inertia. The potential difficulty of this methodology for the present study is as follows: The objective of the inertia measure is to indicate whether or not existing firms are moving to opportunities created by the change occurring within industries. If they are not, the opportunities will be available for exploitation through the formation of new ventures. However, it might take only one or a few non-inertial firms to eliminate available opportunities and destroy the potential for new venture formation. As a result, measuring inertia as an aggregate of individual firm characteristics may not be indicative of all of the industry's existing firms' ability to move to opportunities. In other words, a few non-inertial firms may make up for the extensive inertial characteristics of the rest of the firms in the industry and thereby make the industry as a whole non-inertial, despite the aggregate measures which indicate otherwise.

In summary, average age, average size, and extent of unionization may be problematic measures of inertia in two respects. The implication for this is unfortunate for the present study. Lack of a proper industry-level measure of inertia means that it would be difficult to make conclusions about the relationship, or more appropriately--the lack thereof, between inertia and new venture formations. In short, the operationalization of the inertia variables requires that we view these results as preliminary, and that we may not be able to firmly reject the hypotheses that there is a relationship between inertia and new venture formation. The question obviously needs further investigation, which might be better performed with a qualitative methodology that examines specific incidents of industry change and observes individual firms' responses to those changes and the resultant effect on new venture formations.

Theoretical Implications

Theoretically, this research has taken an Austrian economics viewpoint as a basis for modeling the demand determinants of new venture formations in manufacturing industries. As such, the study explicated the role of industry dynamics in creating disequilibrium and market opportunities for entrepreneurs. Entrepreneurship was viewed as the process of seizing opportunities through the combination of productive inputs. In short, the theory argued that the greater the changes occurring in industries, the greater the opportunities for entrepreneurship and, subsequently, new venture formations. The empirical results provide support for the link between industry change and new venture formations. Industry dynamism does appear to create opportunities for entrepreneurship and new venture formation, and the results provide preliminary support for an Austrian perspective on entrepreneurship. Overall, the results indicate that Austrian and other theoretical perspectives on disequilibrium deserve further attention in entrepreneurial research.

Integrating industrial organization economic theory, the theoretical model has also argued that entry barriers constrain the ability of new ventures to seize upon emerging opportunities. Again, the theoretical model is supported by the empirical analysis, which finds a strong negative relationship between entry barriers and new venture formations. Industrial organization economics perspectives on entry barriers represent an important theoretical foundation for studying venture formations.

Lastly, the theoretical model provides an explanation of the role of organizational inertia in constraining existing firms from moving to emerging opportunities and thereby encouraging new venture formation. The hypothesized positive relationship between industry-level measures of inertia and new venture formations was not borne out in the empirical analysis. The lack of findings, however, may be related more to measurement difficulties than to a lack of a relationship between inertia and new venture formations.

Demand determinants of venture creation. A primary purpose of this study was to test the effect of demand factors on new venture formations. Overall, the empirical results support the contention that demand factors are important determinants of new venture formations in manufacturing industries. The demand factors used in this study were highly related to the rate of new venture formations. The important implication for entrepreneurship research is that demand determinants should be considered in theoretical models and empirical research on venture creations. This validates the recent call of some authors for increased attention to demand determinants and for a "rates" approach to the study of entrepreneurship (Aldrich, 1990; Aldrich & Wiedenmayer, 1991). In addition, emphasis on supply factors and "traits" in prior research needs to be balanced by further investigations into demand determinants.

Industry structural factors. Although the variables in the study are appropriately termed "demand determinants," it is also evident that they represent industry structural variables as defined by industrial organization economists. The strong predictive power of these variables is indicative that industry structure is an important aspect of demand determinants, and more importantly, that it is an important predictor of venture creations and entrepreneurship. As a result, industrial organization economics perspectives are crucial to the understanding of venture creations and should not be overlooked. In fact, the results of this study bring into question the narrow emphasis on psychological and sociological factors in traditional studies of entrepreneurship and ventures creations. Industrial organization economics and the associated concern with industry structure has only recently been recognized and utilized in the entrepreneurship literature (Sandberg, 1986). The present results indicate that economic perspectives and industry structural factors deserve further attention.

LIMITATIONS

Despite the present study's contribution to research on determinants of new venture formations, it does have a number of important limitations. These limitations relate to model specification, measures, data sources, and generalizability. Many of the limitations discussed have important implications for future research.

Model Specification

A number of limitations in the model specification were inherent in the study. First of all, it is entirely possible that a number of important variables could have been left out of the model. The study does not consider supply determinants of new venture formations. While supply determinants might have explained a significant portion of the variance in new venture formations, examining supply determinants was not the purpose of the present research. In addition, most studies of supply determinants investigate variance in new venture creations across regions or societies, rather than across industries. For example, Pennings (1982) investigated the effect of supply factors on rates of new business formations across a sample of urban areas. It is logical to assume that sociological and psychological factors might vary by region or nation. However, it does not make nearly so much sense to think that supply determinants would vary across industries. This is not to rule out the possibility that some variation in supply factors might exist across industries, just that more variance in these factors would occur across regions or societies.

In addition, sources of industry change not included in the present analysis could have an impact on new venture formations. For example, political/regulatory change is not included in the empirical model. In some industries, political and regulatory change has a significant impact on new venture formations. One example is the impact that the airline industry deregulation had on the formation of new airlines such as Peoples Express or Pride Air.

Measures

The measures used in the study could place limits on the implications of the present study. While some measures have a significant history of use as measures of the constructs discussed, others do not. As discussed above, the measures of inertia and niche dynamism were rather innovative and lack a solid empirical history. On the other hand, variables such as advertising, capital requirements, and concentration have been extensively examined in theoretical and empirical research.

Data Sources

Since the study relies on the use of secondary data sources, it is subject to all of the inherent limitations of these sources. One example is that firms do not always immediately enter the USEEM database. Another possible drawback of these sources is the four-digit S.I.C. categorization of industries. Questions have been raised as to whether or not the S.I.C. system represents an appropriate categorization of industries (Scherer, 1980). Potential problems created by the secondary data sources are somewhat mitigated by the fact that all of the sources are used regularly in economic and strategic management research.

Generalizability

This study tested the proposed model on the population of U.S. manufacturing industries in 1978 and 1980. Thus, it provides a valid model for prediction of new venture formations in manufacturing, but its generalizability to other industries is questionable. It is unlikely, for example, that the same variables would operate similarly in service industries. The general theoretical model, however, may still apply. In addition, the empirical analysis revealed that the sample was somewhat biased against highly concentrated industries. Since many of the highly concentrated industries dropped out of the sample due to missing data, the results may not be indicative of the determinants of new venture formations in such industries. Generalizability to other countries' manufacturing sectors may, however, be appropriate. In addition, it is argued that the results should be generalizable to other periods than those studied herein.

Other Limitations

An additional limitation is that the study did not examine the performance of the new ventures created. Sandberg (1986) found that industry structural variables such as that used herein were related to the performance of new ventures. It is possible that the proposed model is indicative of new venture performance as well as rates of formation. For example, industries which are dynamic and have more opportunities may also be those which lead to greater new venture success. Likewise, ventures which do enter industries with high entry barriers may have much more difficulty surviving and becoming profitable.

IMPLICATIONS FOR FUTURE RESEARCH

As with most research, studies such as this imply as many questions as they provide answers. Despite the important findings of the present study, a number of possibilities exist to use the findings as a basis of other studies and to overcome some of the limitations discussed above with alternate research designs.

First, an additional test of the theoretical model could be gained by a fine-grained, qualitative examination. Such a study might be based on a limited number of industries and be based on firm-level data. This approach would allow the identification of specific incidents of industry change and could follow the effect of those changes on existing firms and new ventures. Inertia could be conceptualized as the individual responses of existing firms to the specific change. The formation of individual ventures might be traced to a particular change within the industry.

Future research might also look at the extent to which supply determinants influence new venture formations across industries. Supply factors traditionally have been suggested to vary across societies or regions, but it is possible that certain industry factors create cultures which promote new venture formations. In the electronics industry, for example, certain industry norms which encourage entrepreneurial attitudes might be responsible for higher new venture formations. Trade associations might also have impacts which influence rates of new venture formations. A comparative study which examines the relative effect of supply and demand determinants might be especially interesting. An analysis of specific geographic regions such as the silicon valley, Boston's route 128, the North Carolina Triangle, or the Boulder Valley might shed further light on demand and supply determinants of venture creation. In addition, studies on the corporate spawning of individual entrepreneurs and the creation of genealogies of resultant companies (see for example, Mitton, 1990) might further elucidate the relationships between demand and supply factors.

Within the current theoretical model, researchers may be able to identify additional variables which represent industry dynamism or inertia. Clearly, further research is needed on the nature of inertia and how it might be characterized at the industry level. Other measures of dynamism might also prove useful as predictors of new venture formations. In addition, the use of other sources of data on new venture formations would provide an important verification of the present results.

It may also be appropriate to examine whether some of the variables used in this study might also influence the performance of new ventures. If a venture attempts to enter industries which are highly dynamic and have greater opportunities, that firm may experience superior performance relative to a venture which is formed in a stable industry. Similarly, a venture formed in an industry where existing firms are highly inertial may have a greater probability of long-term survival and profitability. Empirical studies of these relationships could be a useful extension of the current theoretical model.

Finally, the results of the study may or may not apply to non-manufacturing industries. Theoretical or empirical studies which apply the model to service, retail, or other sectors would aid our understanding of new venture formations and how the determinants thereof vary across sectors.

BIBLIOGRAPHY

Acs, Z. J., & Audretsch, D. B. 1989. Small-firm Entry in US Manufacturing. *Economica*, 56: 255-265.

Addison, J. T. 1984. Trade Unions and Restrictive Practices. In J. Rosa (Ed.), *The Economics of Trade Unions: New Directions*: 83-114. Boston: Kluwer Nijhoff Publishing.

Aldrich, H. E. 1979. *Organizations and Environments*. Englewood Cliffs, New Jersey: Prentice Hall.

_____. 1990. Using an Ecological Perspective to Study Organization Founding Rates. *Entrepreneurship Theory and Practice*, 14 (3): 7-24.

Aldrich, H. E., & Wiedenmayer, G. 1991. From Traits to Rates: An Ecological Perspective on Organizational Foundings. In J. Katz & R. Brockhaus (Eds.), *Advances in Entrepreneurship, Firm Emergence, and Growth*: JAI Press.

Aldrich, H. E., Kalleberg, A., Marsden, P., & Cassell, J. 1989. In Pursuit of Evidence: Sampling Procedures for Locating New Businesses. *Journal of Business Venturing*, 4: 367-386.

Applied Systems Inc. 1988. *1976-1986 Linked USEEM Users Guide*. SBA Contract: SBA-2037-OA-87.

Astley, W. G. 1985. The Two Ecologies: Population and Community Perspectives on Organizational Evolution. *Administrative Science Quarterly*, 30: 224-241.

Astley, W. G., & Van de Ven, A. H. 1983. Central Perspectives and Debates in Organization Theory. *Administrative Science Quarterly*, 28: 245-273.

Bain, J. S. 1956. *Barriers to New Competition.* Cambridge, MA: Harvard University Press.

Baron, D. P. 1973. Limit Pricing, Potential Entry, and Barriers to Entry. *American Economic Review*, 63 (4): 666-674.

Baumol, W. J. 1982. Contestable Markets: An Uprising in the Theory of Industry Structure. *American Economic Review*, (March): 1-15.

_____. 1968. Entrepreneurship in Economic Theory. *American Economic Review*, 58 (2): 64-71.

_____. 1986. Entrepreneurship and a Century of Growth. *Journal of Business Venturing*, 1: 141-145.

_____. 1983. Toward Operational Models of Entrepreneurship. In J. Ronen (Ed.), *Entrepreneurship*: 29-48. Lexington, MA: Lexington Books.

Baumol, W. J., Panzar, J. C., & Willig, R. D. 1982. *Contestable Markets and the Theory of Industry Structure.* New York: Harcourt Brace Jovanovich, Inc.

Bedeian, A. G., & Zammuto, R. F. 1991. *Organizations: Theory and Design.* Chicago: Dryden Press.

Bemmels, B. 1987. How Unions Affect Productivity in Manufacturing Plants. *Industrial and Labor Relations Review*, 40 (2): 239-253.

Bhagwati, J. N. 1970. Oligopoly Theory, Entry Prevention, and Growth. *Oxford Economic Papers*, 22: 297-310.

Cohen, J., & Cohen, P. 1983. *Applied Multiple Regression/Correlation Analysis for the Behavioral Sciences.* Hillsdale, NJ: Lawrence Erlbaum Associates.

Birley, S. 1984. Finding the New Firm. *Academy of Management Best Papers Proceedings*, 64-68.

Blau, P. M., & Schoenherr, R. A. 1971. *The Structure of Organizations.* New York: Basic Books.

Blau, P. M. 1956. *Bureaucracy in Modern Society.* New York: Random House.

Boeker, W.P. 1989. Strategic Change: The Effects of Founding and History. *Academy of Management Journal,* 32 (3): 485-488.

_____. 1989. Strategic Change: The Effects of Founding and History. *Academy of Management Journal,* 32 (3): 489-515.

_____. 1988. Organizational Origins: Entrepreneurial and Environmental Imprinting at the Time of Founding. In G. R. Carroll & A.H. Hawley (Eds.), *Ecological Models of Organizations:* 33-51. Cambridge, MA: Ballinger.

Bourgeois, L. J. III 1981. On the Measurement of Organizational Slack. *Academy of Management Review,* 6 (1): 29-39.

Brockhaus, R. H., Horwitz, P. S. 1986. The Psychology of the Entrepreneur. In D. L. Sexton & R. W. Smilor (Eds.), *The Art and Science of Entrepreneurship:* 25-48. Cambridge, MA: Ballinger.

Brockhaus, R. H. 1982. The Psychology of the Entrepreneur. In C. A. Kent, D. L. Sexton, & K. H. Vesper (Eds.), *Encyclopedia of Entrepreneurship:* 39-71. Englewood Cliffs, NJ: Prentice-Hall.

Brown, H. S., & Phillips, B. D. 1989. Comparisons between Small Business Data Base (USEEM) and Bureau of Labor Statistics (BLS) Employment Data: 1978-1986. *Small Business Economics,* 1: 273-28.

Bruno, A. V., & Tyebjee, T. T. 1985. The Entrepreneur's Search for Capital. *Journal of Business Venturing,* 1: 61-74.

Burns, T., Stalker, G. M. 1961. Mechanistic and Organic Systems. In T. Burns & G. M. Stalker, *The Management of Innovation:* 119-125. London: Tavistock Publications.

Carroll, G. R., & Huo, Y. P. 1986. Organizational Task and Institutional Environments in Ecological Perspective: Findings from the Local Newspaper Industry. *American Journal of Sociology*, 91: 838-873.

Carsrud, A. L., Olm, K. W., Eddy, G. G. 1986. Entrepreneurship: Research in Quest of a Paradigm. In D. L. Sexton & R. W. Smilor (Eds.), *The Art and Science of Entrepreneurship*: 367-378. Cambridge, MA: Ballinger.

Caves, R. 1967. *American Industry; Structure, Conduct, Performance*. Englewood Cliffs, NJ: Prentice-Hall.

Caves, R. E., & Porter, M. E. 1976. Barriers to Exit. In R. T. Masson & P. D. Qualls (Eds.), *Essays on Industrial Organization in Honor of Joe S. Bain*: 39-69. Cambridge, MA: Ballinger.

Chakravarthy, B. S. 1986. *Measuring Strategic Performance. Strategic Management Journal*, 7: 437-458.

Chamberlin, E. 1951. Monopolistic Competition Revisited. *Economica*: 343-363.

Chandler, A. D. Jr. 1962. *Strategy and Structure*. Garden City, NY: Doubleday.

Cheah, H. 1990. Schumpeterian and Austrian Entrepreneurship: Unity within Duality. *Journal of Business Venturing*, 5: 341-347.

Child, J. 1972. Organizational Structure, Environment and Performance: The Role of Strategic Choice. *Sociology*, 1: 2-22.

Cochran, T. C. 1971. The Entrepreneur in Economic Change. In Kilby, Peter (Ed.), *Entrepreneurship and Economic Development*: 95-122. New York: The Free Press.

Cohen, W. M., Levin, R. C. 1989. Empirical Studies of Innovation and Market Structure. In R. Schmalensee & R. D. Willig (Eds.), *Handbook of Industrial Organization*: 1059-1107. New York: North-Holland.

Comanor, W. S., & Wilson, T. A. 1967. Advertising Market Structure and Performance. *Review of Economics and Statistics*, 49 (4): 423-440.

Cooper, A. C. 1985. The Role of Incubator Organizations in the Founding of Growth-Oriented Firms. *Journal of Business Venturing*, 1: 75-86.

Cooper, A. C., & Dunkelberg, W. C. 1987. Entrepreneurship Research: Old Questions New Answers, and Methodological Issues. *American Journal of Small Business*, 11 (Winter) (3): 11-23.

Creedy, J., & Johnson, P. S. 1983. Firm Formation in Manufacturing Industry. *Applied Economics*, 15: 177-185.

Cyert, R. M., & March, J. G. 1963. *A Behavioral Theory of the Firm*. Englewood Cliffs, NJ: Prentice Hall.

Dean, J. W. Jr., & Snell, S. A. 1991. Integrated Manufacturing and Job Design: Moderating Effects of Organizational Inertia. *Academy of Management Journal*, 34 (4): 776-804.

Delacroix, J., & Carroll, G. R. 1983. Organizational Foundings: An Ecological Study of the Newspaper Industries of Argentina and Ireland. *Administrative Science Quarterly*, 28: 274-291.

Demsetz, H. 1982. Barriers to Entry. *American Economic Review*, 72 (March): 47-57.

Dess, G. G., & Beard, D. W. 1984. Dimensions of Organizational Task Environments. *Administrative Science Quarterly*, 29: 52-73.

Duetsch, L. L. 1975. Structure, Performance, and the Net Rate of Entry into Manufacturing Industries. *Southern Economic Journal*, 41: 450-456.

DiMaggio, P. J., & Powell, W. W. 1983. The Iron Cage Revisited: Institutional Isomorphism and Collective Rationality in Organizational Fields. *American Sociological Review*, 48: 147-160.

Dixit, A. 19ℝ82, A. 1982. Recent Developments in Oligopoly Theory. *American Economic Review*, 72 (May) (2): 12-17.

Downs, A. 1967. *Inside Bureaucracy*. Boston: Little Brown.

Drucker, P. F. 1985. The Discipline of Innovation. *Harvard Business Review*, (May-June): 67-72.

Duncan, R. B. 1972. Characteristics of Organizational Environments and Perceived Environmental Uncertainty. *Administrative Science Quarterly*, 17 (3): 313-327.

Elbing, A. O. 1974. On the Applicability of Environmental Models. In J. M. McGuire (Ed.), *Contemporary Management: Issues and Viewpoints*: 283-289. Englewood Cliffs, NJ: Prentice Hall.

Emery, F. E., & Trist, E. L. 1965. The Causal Texture of Organizational Environments. *Human Relations*, 18: 21-32.

Flanagan, R. J. 1990. The Economics of Unions and Collective Bargaining. *Industrial Relations*, 29 (2): 300-315.

Florida, R., & Kenney, M. 1988. Venture Capital and High Technology Entrepreneurship. *Journal of Business Venturing*, 3: 301-319.

Frederickson, J. W., & Iaquinto, A. L. 1989. Inertia and Creeping Rationality in Strategic Decision Processes. *Academy of Management Journal*, 32 (3): 516-542.

Freeman, R. B., & Medhoff, J. L. 1979. New Estimates of Private Sector Unionism in the United States. *Industrial and Labor Relations Review*, 32: 143-174.

Gartner, W. B. 1988. "Who Is an Entrepreneur?" Is the Wrong Question. *American Journal of Small Business*, 2 (4): 11-31.

_____. 1989. Some Suggestions for Research on Entrepreneurial Traits and Characteristics. *Entrepreneurship Theory and Practice*, 14 (1): 27-37.

_____. 1990. What Are We Talking about when We Talk about Entrepreneurship. *Journal of Business Venturing*, 5: 15-28.

Geroski, P., Gilbert, R. J., & Jacquemin, A. 1990. *Barriers to Entry and Strategic Competition.* New York: Harwood Academic Publishers.

Gilad, B. 1982. On Encouraging Entrepreneurship: An Interdisciplinary Analysis. *Journal of Behavioral Economics,* 11: 132-163.

Gilbert, R. J. 1989. Mobility Barriers and the Value of Incumbency. In R. Schmalensee (Ed.), *Handbook of Industrial Organization*: 475-535. New York: North-Holland.

Glade, W. P. 1967. Approaches to a Theory of Entrepreneurial Formation. *Explorations in Entrepreneurial History,* 4 (3): 245-259.

Glass, G. V., & Hopkins, K. D. 1984. *Statistical Methods in Education and Psychology.* Englewood Cliffs, NJ: Prentice-Hall.

Gorecki, P. K. 1975. The Determinants of Entry by New and Diversifying Enterprises in the UK Manufacturing Sector 1958-1963: Some Tentative Results. *Applied Economics,* 7: 139-147.

Greenfield, S. M., & Strickon, A. 1981. A New Paradigm for the Study of Entrepreneurship and Social Change. *Economic Development,* 29: 467-499.

Hagen, E. 1962. *On the Theory of Social Change: How Economic Growth Begins.* Homewood, IL:

Hambrick, D. C. 1989. Guest Editors Introduction: Putting Managers Back in the Strategy Picture. *Strategic Management Journal,* 10: 5-16.

_____. 1982. Environmental scanning and Organizational Strategy. *Strategic Management Journal,* 3: 159-174.

Hamilton, R. T. 1985. Interindustry Variation in Gross Entry Rates of 'independent' and 'dependent' businesses. *Applied Economics,* 17: 271-280.

Hannan, M. T., & Freeman, J. H. 1977. The Population Ecology of Organizations. *American Journal of Sociology,* 82: 929-964.

_____. 1984. Structural Inertia and Organizational Change. *American Journal of Sociology*, 89: 149-164.

_____. 1987. The ecology of Organizational Foundings: American Labor Unions, 1836-1985. *American Journal of Sociology*, 92 (4): 910-943.

Harrigan, K. R. 1985. *Strategic Flexibility*. Lexington, MA: Lexington Books.

_____. 1983a. Entry Barriers in Mature Manufacturing Industries. *Advances in Strategic Management*, 2: 67-97.

_____. 1983b. Research Methodologies for Contingency Approaches to Business Strategy. *Academy of Management Review*, 8 (3): 398-405.

_____. 1980. The Effect of Exit Barriers Upon Strategic Flexibility. *Strategic Management Journal*, 1: 165-176.

_____. 1981. Barriers to Entry and Competitive Strategies. *Strategic Management Journal*, 2: 395-412.

Harris, M. N. 1976. Entry and Barriers to Entry. *Industrial Organization Review*, 4: 165-174.

Hatten, K., & Hatten, M. 1987. Strategic Groups, Asymmetrical Mobility Barriers, and Contestability. *Strategic Management Journal*, 8 (4): 329-342.

Hause, J. C., & Du Reitz, G. 1984. Entry, Industry Growth, and the Microdynamics of Industry Supply. *Journal of Political Economy*, 92 (4): 733-757.

Hayek, F. A. 1948. *Individualism and Economic Order*. Chicago, IL: University of Chicago Press.

Highfield, R., & Smiley, R. 1987. New Business Start and Economic Activity: An Empirical Investigation. *International Journal of Industrial Organization*, 5: 51-66.

Hilke, J. C. 1984. Excess Capacity and Entry: Some Empirical Evidence. *The Journal of Industrial Economics*, 33 (2): 233-240.

Hisrich, R. D. 1988. Entrepreneurship: Past, Present, and Future. *Journal of Small Business Management*, 26 (October) (4): 1-4.

Hornaday, J. A., Chuchill, N. C. 1987. Current Trends in Entrepreneurial Research. In N. C. Churchill, J. A. Hornaday, B. A. Kirchoff, O. J. Krasner, & K. H. Vesper (Eds.), *Frontiers of Entrepreneurship Research*: 1-21. Wellesley, MA Babson College.

Hrebiniak, L. G., & Snow, C. C. 1980. Industry Differences in Environmental Uncertainty and Organizational Characteristics Related to Uncertainty. *Academy of Management Journal*, 23: 750-759.

Hughes, K. 1988. The Interpretation and Measurement of R&D Intensity - A Note. *Research Policy*, 17: 301-307.

Katz, D., & Kahn, R. L. 1966. *The Social Psychology of Organizations*. New York: John Wiley.

Keats, B. W., & Hitt, M. A. 1988. A Causal Model of Linkages among Environmental Dimensions, Macro Organizational Characteristics, and Performance. *Academy of Management Journal*, 31 (3): 570-598.

Kessides, I. N. 1986. Advertising, Sunk Costs, and Barriers to Entry. *Review of Economics and Statistics*, 68: 84-95.

Khemani, R. S., & Shapiro, D. M. 1986. The Determinants of Plant Entry in Canada. *Applied Economics*, 18: 1243-1257.

Kilby, P. 1971. Hunting the Heffalump. In P. Kilby (Ed.), *Entrepreneurship and Economic Development*: 1-40. New York: The Free Press.

Kim, J., Kohut, F. J. 1975. Multiple Regression Analysis: Subprogram Regression. In N. H. Nie, C. H. Hull, J. G. Jenkins, K. Steinbrenner, & D. H. Bent (Eds.), SPSS: *Statistical Package for the Social Sciences*: 320-367. New York: McGraw Hill.

Kirzner, I. M. 1979. Comment: X-Inefficiency, Error, and the Scope for Entrepreneurship. In M. J. Rizzo (Ed.), *Time, Uncertainty, and Disequilibrium: Exploration of Austrian Themes*: 141-151. Lexington, MA: Lexington Books.

_____. 1983. Entrepreneurs and the Entrepreneurial Function: A Commentary. In J. Ronen (Ed.), *Entrepreneurship*: 281-290. Lexington, MA: Lexington Books.

_____. 1973. *Competition and Entrepreneurship*. Chicago: The University of Chicago Press.

Knight, F. H. 1921. *Risk, Uncertainty and Profit*. Boston: Houghton Mifflin.

Kochan, T. A., McKersie, R. B., & Cappelli, P. 1984. Strategic Choice and Industrial Relations Theory. *Industrial Relations*, 23 (1): 16-39.

Kokkelenberg, E. C., & Sockell, D. R. 1985. Union Membership in the United States, 1973-1981. *Industrial and Labor Relations Review*, 38 (4): 497-543.

Kunkel, S. W., & Hofer, C. W. 1991. Ease of Entry: A Step Beyond Entry Barriers. *Proceedings to the U.S. Association for Small Business and Entrepreneurship 6th Annual National Conference*: 6-15.

Lawrence, P. R., & Lorsch, J. W. 1967. Differentiation and Integration in Complex Organizations. *Administrative Science Quarterly*, 12 (1): 1-47.

Leibenstein, H. 1968. Entrepreneurship and Development. *American Economic Review*, 58: 72-83.

_____. 1979. The General X-Efficiency Paradigm and the Role of the Entrepreneur. In M. J. Rizzo (Ed.), *Time, Uncertainty, and Disequilibrium*: 127-139. Lexington, Mass: D. C. Heath.

_____, H. 1966. Allocative Efficiency vs. X-Efficiency. *American Economic Review*, 56 (3): 392-415.

Lieberman, M. B. 1987. Excess Capacity as a Barrier to Entry: An Empirical Appraisal. *The Journal of Industrial Economics*, 35 (4): 607-627.

Long, W. 1983. The Meaning of Entrepreneurship. *American Journal of Small Business*, 8 (2): 47-56.

Low, M. B., & MacMillan, I. C. 1988. Entrepreneurship: Past Research and Future Challenges. *Journal of Management*, 14 (2): 139-161.

Macdonald, J. M. 1986. Entry and Exit on the Competitive Fringe. *Southern Economic Journal*, 52 (3): 640-652.

Mansfield, E. 1962. Entry, Gibrat's Law, Innovation, and the Growth of Firms. *The American Economic Review*, 52: 1023-1050.

March, J. G., & Simon, H. A. 1958. *Organizations*. New York: John Wiley.

Marshall, A. 1890. *Principles of Economics*. London: MacMillan.

Maurice, S. C., & Smithson, C. W. 1985. *Managerial Economics*. Homewood, IL: Irwin.

McClelland, D. C. 1961. *The Achieving Society*. Princeton, NJ: D. Van Nostrand.

McGee, J. 1985. Strategic Groups: A Bridge Between Industry Structure and Strategic Management. In H. Thomas & D. Gardner, *Strategic Marketing and Management*: NY: Wiley.

McGuckin, R. 1972. Entry, Concentration Change, and Stability of Market Shares. *Southern Economic Journal*, 38 (January): 363-370.

Merton, R. K. 1949. *Social Theory and Social Structure*. Glencoe, IL: Free Press.

Miles, R. E., Snow, Charles C., & Pfeffer, J. 1974. Organization-Environment: Concepts and Issues. *Industrial Relations*, 13: 244-264.

Miller, D., & Friesen, P. H. 1980. Momentum and Revolution in Organizational Adaptation. *Academy of Management Journal*, 23: 591-614.

Mises, L. 1949. *Human Action: A Treatise on Economics*. Chicago: Henry Regnery.

Mitton, Daryl G. 1990. *Bring on the Clones: A Longitudinal Study of the Proliferation, Development, and Growth of the Biotech Industry in San Diego*. Paper presented at the Babson Entrepreneurship Research Conference, Wellesley, MA.

Nelson, R. R., & Winter, S. G. 1982. *An Evolutionary Theory of Economic Change*. Cambridge, MA: Belknap Press of Harvard University Press.

Neter, J., Wasserman, W., & Kutner, M. H. 1983. *Applied Linear Regression Models*. Homewood, IL: Richard D. Irwin, Inc.

Nightingale, J. 1978. On the Definition of 'Industry' and 'Market'. *The Journal of Industrial Economics*, 27 (September) (1): 31-40.

Norusis, M. J. 1990. *SPSS Base System Users Guide*. Chicago, IL: SPSS, Inc.

Orr, D. 1974. The Determinants of Entry: A Study of the Canadian Manufacturing Industries. *Review of Economics and Statistics*, 56: 58-66.

Pennings, J. M. 1982. Organizational Birth Frequencies: An Empirical Investigation. *Administrative Science Quarterly*, 27: 120-144.

_____. 1980. Environmental Influences on the Creation Process. In J. R. Kimberly & R. H. Miles (Eds.), *The Organizational Life Cycle*: 134-160. San Francisco, CA: Jossey-Bass.

Penrose, E. T. 1963. *The Theory of the Growth of the Firm*. Oxford: Basil Blackwell.

Pfeffer, J., & Salancik, G. R. 1978. *The External Control of Organizations: A Resource Dependence Perspective*. New York: Harper & Row.

Porter, M. E. 1980. *Competitive Strategy.* New York: Free Press.

_____. 1985. *Competitive Advantage.* NY: Basic Books.

_____. 1981. The Contributions of Industrial Organization to Strategic Management. *Academy of Management Review,* 6 (4): 609-620.

Pugh, D. S., Hickson, D. J., Hinings, C. R., & Turner, C. 1969. The Context of Organizations. *Administrative Science Quarterly,* 14 (1): 91-114.

Rees, A. 1962. *The Economics of Trade Unions.* Chicago: The University of Chicago Press.

Reynolds, P. D., West, S., Finch, M. D. 1985. Estimating New Firms and New Jobs: Considerations in Using the Dun and Bradstreet Files. In J. A. Hornaday, E. B. Shils, J. A. Timmons, & K. H. Vesper (Eds.), *Frontiers of Entrepreneurship Research*: 383-399. Wellesley, MA Babson College.

Rizzo, M. J. 1979. Disequilibrium and All That: An Introductory Essay. In M. J. Rizzo (Ed.), *Time, Uncertainty, and Disequilibrium: Exploration of Austrian Themes*: 1-18. Lexington, MA: Lexington Books.

Romanelli, E. 1989. Organizational Birth and Population Variety. *Research in Organizational Behavior,* 11: 211-246.

Romanelli, E., & Tushman, M. L. 1986. Inertia, Environments, and Strategic Choice: A Quasi-Experimental Design for Comparative Longitudinal Research. *Management Science,* 32 (5): 608-621.

Rosen, S. 1983. Economics and Entrepreneurs. In J. Ronen (Ed.), *Entrepreneurship*: 301-311. Lexington, MA: Lexington Books.

Rumelt, R. 1987. Theory, Strategy, and Entrepreneurship. In D. J. Teece (Ed.), *The Competitive Challenge*: 137-158.Ballinger.

Sandberg, W. R. 1986. *New Venture Performance: The Role of Strategy and Industry Structure.* Lexington, MA: Lexington Books.

Say, J. B. 1803. *A Treatise on Political Economy: Or, The Production, Distribution and Consumption of Wealth.* New York: Augustus M. Kelley.

Scherer, F. M. 1980. *Industrial Market Structure and Economic Performance.* Chicago: Rand McNally.

Scherer, F. M., & Ross, D. 1990. *Industrial Market Structure and Economic Performance.* Boston: Houghton Mifflin Company.

Schmalensee, R. 1988. Industrial Economics: An Overview. *The Economic Journal,* 98 (September): 643-681.

Schultz, T. W. 1975. The Value of the Ability to Deal with Disequilibrium. *Journal of Economic Literature,* 13 (2): 827-846.

Schumpeter, J. 1934. The Business Cycle. In J. Schumpeter, *The Theory of Economic Development*: 212-255. Cambridge, MA: Harvard University Press.

Sexton, D. L., Smilor, R. W. 1986. Introduction. In D. L. Sexton & R. W. Smilor (Eds.), *The Art and Science of Entrepreneurship*: Cambridge, MA: Ballinger.

Sexton, D. L. 1987. Advancing Small Business Research: Utilizing Research from other Areas. *American Journal of Small Business,* 11 (Winter) (3): 25-30.

_____. 1988. The Field of Entrepreneurship: Is It Growing or Just Getting Bigger. *Journal of Small Business Management,* 26 (January): 5-8.

Shapero, A., Sokol, L. 1982. The Social Dimensions of Entrepreneurship. In C. A. Kent, D. L. Sexton, K. H. Vesper (Eds.), *Encyclopedia of Entrepreneurship*: 73-90. Englewood Cliffs, NJ: Prentice-Hall.

Shapiro, D., & Khemani, R. S. 1987. The Determinants of Entry and Exit Reconsidered. *International Journal of Industrial Organization,* 5: 15-26.

Singh, J. V. (Ed.) 1990. *Organizational Evolution-New Directions*. Newbury Park: Sage Publications.

Singh, J. V., House, R. J., & Tucker, D. J. 1986. Organizational Change and Organizational Mortality. *Administrative Science Quarterly*, 31: 587-611.

Spence, A. M. 1977. Entry, Capacity, Investment, and Oligopolistic Pricing. *The Bell Journal of Economics*, 8 (2): 534-544.

_____. 1980. Notes on Advertising, Economies of Scale, and Entry Barriers. *Quarterly Journal of Economics*, 95 (November): 493-507.

Star, A. D., & Narayana, C. L. 1983. Do We Really Know the Number of Small Business Starts? *Journal of Small Business Management*, 21 (October): 44-48.

Starbuck, W. H. 1983. Organizations and Their Environments. In M. D. Dunnette (Ed.) *Handbook of Industrial and Organizational Psychology*: 1069-1123. New York: John Wiley & Sons.

Stigler, G. J. 1968. *The Organization of Industry*. Homewood, IL: Irwin.

Stinchcombe, A. L. 1965. Social Structure and Organizations. In J. G. March, *Handbook of Organizations*: 142-193. Chicago: Rand McNally.

Terreberry, S. 1968. The Evolution of Organizational Environments. *Administrative Science Quarterly*, 12: 590-613.

Thompson, J. D. 1967. *Organizations in Action*. New York: McGraw-Hill.

Timmons, J. A. 1990. *Venture Creation: Entrepreneurship in the 1990's*. Homewood, IL: Irwin.

_____. 1982. New Venture Creation: Models and Methodologies. In C. A. Kent, D. L. Sexton, & K. H. Vesper (Eds.), *Encyclopedia of Entrepreneurship*: 126-139. Englewood Cliffs, NJ: Prentice-Hall.

Timmons, J. A., & Bygrave, W. D. 1986. Venture Capital's Role in Financing Innovation for Economic Growth. *Journal of Business Venturing*, 1: 161-176.

Triffin, R. 1939. *Monopolistic Competition and General Equilibrium Theory*. Cambridge, Mass: Harvard University Press.

Tucker, D. J., Singh, J. V., & Meinhard, Agnes G. 1990. Organizational From, Population Dynamics, and Institutional Change: The Founding Patterns of Voluntary Organizations. *Academy of Management Journal*, 33 (1): 151-178.

Tucker, D. J., Singh, J. V., Meinhard, A. G., House, R. J. 1988. Ecological and Institutional Sources of Change in Organizational Populations. In G. R. Carroll & A. H. Hawley (Eds.), *Ecological Models of Organizations*: 127-151. Cambridge, MA: Ballinger.

Tushman, M., & Anderson, P. 1986. Technological Discontinuities and Organizational Environments. *Administrative Science Quarterly*, 31: 439-465.

Tushman, M. L., Romanelli, E. 1985. Organizational Evolution: A Metamorphisis Model of Convergence and Reorientation. In L. L. Cummings & B. M. Staw (Eds.), *Research in Organizational Behavior*: 223-262. Greenwich, Conn.: JAI Press.

U.S. Department of Commerce, Office of Management and Budget. *1972 Standard Industrial Classification Manual*.

_____. *1977 Supplement to the 1972 Standard Industrial Classification Manual*.

U.S. Department of Commerce, Bureau of the Census. 1986. *1982 Census of Manufactures: General Summary*. MC82-S-1.

_____. 1977. *1976 Annual Survey of Manufactures: Value of Product Shipments*. M76(AS)-2.

_____. *1971 Annual Survey of Manufactures: Value of Product Shipments*.

_____. 1981. *1977 Census of Manufactures: Subject Statistics*.

_____. *Survey of Plant Capacity, 1977.* MQ-C1(77)-1.

_____. 1986. *Concentration Ratios in Manufacturing.* MC82-S-7.

U.S. Federal Trade Commission, Bureau of Economics. *Statistical Report: Annual Line of Business Report, 1977.*

_____. *Statistical Report: Annual Line of Business Report, 1976.*

_____. 1981. *Statistical Report: Annual Line of Business Report, 1975.*

_____. 1981. *Statistical Report: Annual Line of Business Report, 1974.*

U.S. Small Business Administration, Office of Advocacy. 1988. *Uses and Limitations of USEEM/USELM Data.*

_____. 1988. 88-600379 *Handbook of Small Business Data.*

_____. 1988. *The Small Business Database: A Users Guide.*

VanderWerf, P. A., & Brush, C. G. 1989. Achieving Empirical Progress in an Undefined Field. *Entrepreneurship Theory and Practice,* 14 (2): 45-58.

von Weizsacker, C. C. 1980. *Barriers to Entry.* Berlin: Springer-Verlag.

Weber, M. 1930. *The Protestant Ethic and the Spirit of Capitalism.* New York: Scribners.

Weick, K. 1977. *The Social Psychology of Organizing.* Reading, Massachusetts: Addison-Wesley.

Wenders, J. T. 1971. Excess Capacity as a Barrier to Entry. *Journal of Industrial Economics,* 20 (November): 14-19.

Wholey, D. R., & Brittain, J. W. 1989. Characterizing Environmental Variation. *Academy of Management Journal,* 32 (4): 867-882.

_____. 1986. Organizational Ecology: Findings and Implications. *Academy of Management Review*, 11 (3): 513-533.

Williamson, O. 1963. Selling Expense as a Barrier to Entry. *Quarterly Journal of Economics*, 77: 115-128.

Winn, D. N. 1975. *Industrial Market Structure and Performance: 1960-1968*. Ann Arbor, MI: The University of Michigan.

Winter, S. G. 1990. Survival, Selection and Inheritance in Evolutionary Theories of Organization. In J. V. Singh (Ed.), *Organizational Evolution: New Directions*: 269-297. Newbury Park: Sage Publications.

Wortman, M. S., Jr. 1987. Entrepreneurship: An Integrated Typology and Evaluation of the Empirical Research in the Field. *Journal of Management*, 13 (Summer) (2): 259-279.

Yip, G.. S. 1982. *Barriers to Entry: A Corporate Strategy Perspective*. Lexington, MA: Lexington Books.

Zammuto, R. F. 1988. Organizational Adaptation: Some Implications of Organizational Ecology for Strategic Choice. *Journal of Management Studies*, 25 (2): 105-120.

INDEX

Acs 7, 58, 62-67, 69, 79, 92, 101, 112, 118, 121, 123, 162, 164, 165, 169
adapt 14, 43, 44, 49, 50, 83
adaptation 46, 47
Addison 96, 100
advertising 55-58, 68, 93, 94, 102-106, 110, 113, 119, 120, 123, 126, 131, 147, 149, 159, 164, 167-169, 173
advertising intensity 68, 93, 94, 102-106, 113, 119, 120, 123, 126, 131, 147, 149, 159, 164, 167-169
Aldrich 4-6, 11, 41, 42, 48, 49, 112, 113, 172
alertness 6, 22, 37, 74, 85
Annual Survey of Manufactures 110, 113, 116, 123
Applied 7, 10, 17, 53, 70
assumptions 7, 9, 16-18, 21, 23, 43, 73, 107, 125, 151, 153, 158, 159, 169
Astley 44, 46, 51, 83, 96-98
Austrian economic 8, 33, 88
Austrian Economics 9, 21, 34, 71, 171
Austrian economists 8, 15, 16, 21, 22, 30, 34, 44

Bain 7, 8, 53-55, 58, 59, 61, 93-95
Baron 64
barriers 7-10, 14, 31-33, 35, 47, 49, 52-57, 59, 61, 62, 64, 67, 68, 69-72, 81-83, 89, 92, 93, 102, 103, 105, 106, 119, 123, 126, 147, 149, 159, 161-163, 165-167, 171, 174
Baumol 4, 6, 7, 16, 17, 54, 56, 61
Bedeian 19, 43, 46, 77, 90, 91
Bemmels 96, 100
Bhagwati 64
Birley 111, 112
Blau 45, 97, 99
Boeker 46, 47, 49, 97, 98
Brockhaus 3, 4, 10
Brown 107, 111, 112
Bruno 6
bureaucracy 44, 97, 99
bureaucratic 40, 45, 97
Burns 40, 43, 91
business formations 5-7, 10, 15, 38, 57, 81, 173
capacity utilization 33, 35, 59, 60, 76, 102, 119, 120

capital requirements 59,
61-63, 93, 95, 102-106,
113, 119, 120, 121, 123,
126, 131, 144, 147, 149,
150, 159, 164, 167, 173
Carroll 4, 7, 51, 77
Carsrud 4
causality 161
Caves 54, 58, 165
Census of Manufactures
109-111, 113, 116, 120,
121
Chamberlin 19, 20, 23
Chandler 99
Cheah 4, 38, 86, 88
Child 41-43, 46
Cochran 6
Cohen 93, 117, 118
Comanor 55, 56, 93, 94
community ecology 51, 97,
98
competition 18-20, 94
complete information 18, 20,
29
complete markets 29
complexity 41, 42, 50, 97,
99
concentration 4, 5, 55,
63-65, 70, 93, 95,
102-106, 108-110, 113,
119, 121, 123, 126, 131,
147, 149, 150, 159, 164,
167, 168, 173
constraints 19, 47, 49, 50,
72, 80-83, 102, 163
constraints on existing firms
72, 80-82, 102, 163
consumers 13, 17-21, 39, 40,
55, 56, 75, 76, 90, 101
contestable market 61
Cooper 4, 92, 165

creation of new ventures 16,
38, 115, 163, 167
Creedy 7
cross-price elasticity 18
Dean 99, 170
Delacroix 4, 7, 51, 77
demand 6-9, 12, 13, 15,
17-21, 23, 27-29, 32,
33, 39, 60, 68, 70, 71,
74, 76, 84, 85, 89-92,
100-102, 116, 117, 171,
172, 175
demand curve 13, 18, 20,
39, 76
Demand determinants 6-9,
15, 70, 71, 171, 172,
175
demand growth 89-91, 102
demand volatility 91, 102,
117
Demsetz 55, 56, 62
density dependence 48
Dess 41, 42, 91, 116, 117,
166
determinants of business
formations 5-7, 15
differentiation 19, 20, 23,
54-56, 68, 70, 93, 94,
99, 164, 169
DiMaggio 50
disequilibrator 28, 85, 88
disequilibria 32, 36, 37, 42,
85
disequilibrium 8, 9, 12,
14-16, 21, 22, 24-26,
28, 30, 32-38, 52, 68,
70-76, 78, 79, 82,
84-88, 92, 98, 101, 163,
167, 171
distribution 54, 55, 61, 68,
69, 94, 104, 117, 125,
129-132, 153, 154, 162

Dixit 60, 61, 168
Downs 99
Drucker 3
Duetsch 63-67, 90, 95, 114,
115, 119, 121, 168
Duncan 42, 75, 91
dynamic change 27, 37, 39
dynamic industries 8
dynamic markets 8, 28, 71
dynamics of industries 15,
36, 38
dynamics of markets 21, 34,
39
dynamism 16, 38, 41-43,
73-80, 82, 89-91,
101-106, 113, 115, 116,
117, 123, 126, 129, 144,
147, 148, 159, 163-167,
169, 171, 173, 175
economic actors 14, 22, 34,
36, 37, 73, 101
Economic Development 3, 4,
37, 80, 87
economic equilibrium 17
economic growth 3, 16, 17,
31, 85, 87
economic profit 18, 36, 73,
80, 166
economic system 6, 10, 11,
22, 31, 32, 84
Economics 8, 9, 17, 18, 21,
29, 34, 41, 43, 44, 52,
64, 70, 71, 89, 93, 167,
171, 172
economies of scale 54-61,
70, 94, 95
economist 17, 24, 52, 57
elasticity 18, 20
Elbing 41
Emery 41-43, 91

entrant 31, 33, 35, 53, 54,
56, 58-61, 63-68, 82,
85, 94, 115, 167
Entrepreneur 3-5, 7, 8, 11,
12, 16-18, 21-29, 31,
35-38, 47, 84, 85-88
entrepreneurial ability 32, 85
entrepreneurial activity 5-7,
15, 26, 27, 30-32, 35,
78-80, 85, 102
entrepreneurial profit 24, 25,
27
entrepreneurial rent 12
Entrepreneurship research
8-10, 171
entry 7-11, 14, 15, 31-35,
47, 49, 52-72, 81-83,
85, 89-95, 101, 102,
103, 105-107, 110, 114,
115, 118, 119, 120, 121,
123, 126, 144, 147, 149,
159, 161, 162-169, 171,
174
entry barriers 7-10, 14, 33,
35, 47, 52-56, 59, 61,
64, 68-72, 81-83, 89,
93, 102, 103, 105, 106,
119, 123, 126, 147, 149,
159, 161-163, 166, 167,
171, 174
entry gateways 68-70
entry measure 57
entry theory 10
Environment 12, 14, 35, 38,
40-44, 46, 48, 49, 51,
63, 75, 83, 91, 98, 100,
166
environmental change 40,
43, 45-47, 50, 98-100
environmental complexity
41, 42

environmental dynamism 41-43, 75, 91, 166
environmental factors 8
environmental munificence 166, 167
environmental variation 42, 44, 49, 50
equilibrium 7, 16, 17, 21-24, 26, 28, 30, 34-37, 39, 73, 74, 77, 85-88, 102
equilibrium theory 7, 16, 17, 23
excess capacity 59, 60, 93-95, 103-106, 120, 123, 126, 131, 147, 149, 159, 164, 167, 168
exit 33, 49, 76, 114
Flanagan 99, 100
Florida 93, 165
founding rates 6, 51
Foundings 5, 6, 48, 49, 51, 53, 70
Frederickson 46
Freeman 4, 7, 14, 44, 46-52, 83, 96-98, 100, 110, 111, 122, 123
gap filling 26, 35, 36
gaps 25, 26, 35-37
Gartner 4, 5, 10, 11
general equilibrium 7, 16, 17, 21, 23
Geroski 52, 53, 59
Gilad 6, 85
Gilbert 14, 52, 54, 55, 58, 59, 83, 94
Glade 6, 7
Glass 158
Gorecki 54, 58, 64, 66, 83, 89, 90, 119
Greenfield 17
gross entry 57, 58, 62-67, 69, 114

Hagen 6
Hambrick 43, 46, 75
Hamilton 62-67, 114, 162, 164, 167, 168
Hannan 4, 7, 14, 44, 46-52, 83, 96-98
Harrigan 7, 58, 60, 62-66, 90, 107, 121, 169
Harris 58, 62-67, 119, 166
Hatten 20, 90, 165
Hause 66, 90, 115
Hayek 7, 17, 18, 73
heterogeneous demand 18-20, 27, 28, 39, 71, 84
heterogeneous markets 18
Highfield 7, 58, 62-67, 69, 89, 90, 92, 95, 112, 121, 162, 164, 166, 169
Hilke 60
Hisrich 3, 4
homogeneous demand 23
homogeneous markets 18
homoscedasticity 154, 156
Hrebiniak 38
Hughes 93
human tastes 22, 23, 36, 39, 76
ignorance 22, 35, 37, 43, 47
imperfect market 26
imperfections 26
incomplete information 18, 26, 74
incomplete markets 34-36, 40
increases in demand 13, 76, 89
incumbent 14, 31, 35, 37, 47, 54, 56, 60-63, 69, 70, 83, 94, 95
inducement 89

industrial organization 8-10, 15, 34, 52, 53, 57, 64, 70, 71, 89, 93, 94, 167, 171, 172

Industrial organization economic 171

industrial organization economist 52, 57

industry 4, 8-16, 18-20, 27-29, 31, 33, 35, 38, 39, 43, 44, 47, 52, 53-61, 63-84, 87, 89-96, 98-103, 105, 106, 108-110, 113-123, 128, 131, 147-150, 159, 161-175

industry change 13, 38, 39, 43, 70, 72, 74, 75, 78, 79, 81, 170, 171, 173, 175

industry concentration 63-65, 70, 93, 95, 102, 103, 110, 113, 119, 121, 123, 131, 150, 159, 164, 167, 168

industry dynamics 8, 9, 16, 38, 39, 43, 52, 70-72, 75, 161, 163, 171

industry dynamism 16, 38, 73-80, 89, 102, 103, 105, 106, 115, 123, 147, 148, 159, 163, 166, 167, 171, 175

industry environment 38, 63

industry profitability 65, 67, 79

industry structure 57, 172

inertia 8-10, 14-16, 25, 35, 38, 44-50, 52, 56, 70-72, 81-85, 89, 96-103, 105, 106, 121, 123, 126, 144, 147, 150, 159, 161, 163, 169-171, 173, 175

inertial 8, 14, 15, 37, 38, 44, 46, 47, 49, 50, 82-85, 96, 97, 100, 102, 170, 176

input completing 26, 35, 36

institutional change 51, 52

institutionalization 50

invention 30, 86-88

Katz 40

Keats 96, 99, 170

Kessides 56

Khemani 57, 58, 62-67, 69, 79, 104, 107, 120, 131, 167

Kilby 4, 6

Kim 117

Kirzner 4, 6, 7, 10, 11, 14, 16-18, 21-25, 27, 34-37, 39, 43, 47, 71, 73, 74, 76, 77, 79, 83-88

Knight 7, 10, 16-18, 21, 24, 25, 27, 28, 35-37, 39, 43, 71, 73, 74, 76, 166

Kochan 100

Kokkelenberg 123

Kunkel 69, 94, 168

large scale entry 64

large-scale entry 58-60

Lawrence 41

Leibenstein 7, 14, 16-18, 21, 25-27, 34-37, 43, 45-47, 71, 83, 84

Lieberman 60

limit price 59

Line of Business Data 109-111, 113, 123

linearity 129, 132, 151-153, 158

Long 3, 10, 36, 87, 89, 100, 107, 112, 176

Low 3, 4, 22, 44, 48, 59, 60, 84, 112, 125, 132

Macdonald 57, 58, 62, 63, 66, 67, 90, 112, 119, 164, 167, 169

Management 4, 19, 20, 22, 33, 34, 40, 43, 44, 46, 100, 174

Mansfield 62, 63, 67

March 44, 45, 99

market 8-18, 20-29, 31-40, 42, 43, 47, 52-54, 58, 60, 61, 63, 65, 66, 67, 69-90, 92-94, 101-103, 107, 108, 115, 164, 171

market change 13, 16, 23, 24, 28, 35, 36, 75, 76

market disequilibrium 8, 14, 15, 22, 25, 34, 35, 52, 73, 75, 92

market dynamics 9, 13, 15, 22, 27, 36, 37, 40, 76

market equilibrium 22, 35, 85

market gaps 35-37

market growth 33, 164

market opportunities 10, 11, 14, 22-24, 27, 28, 31, 34, 36-38, 43, 47, 70, 72-75, 77, 78, 80-85, 101, 102, 171

market opportunity 14-16, 26, 28, 35, 39, 73-75, 77-80, 89, 107

market performance 53

market process 22-24, 39, 84

Marshall 39

Maurice 12, 13, 20, 39

McClelland 3, 6

McGee 18, 20

McGuckin 114, 115

measure of entry 57, 58, 63-67, 69

measures of entry 55, 62, 115

Merton 45, 99

Miles 40, 43

Miller 14, 45, 46, 83

Mises 7, 11, 15, 17, 21, 24, 34-37, 71, 73, 74, 77

Mitton 92, 165, 175

modification of demand 13, 76, 89, 90

monopoly 20, 26

multicollinearity 151, 157, 158, 167

munificence 41, 166, 167

Nelson 96

neoclassical 17, 18, 21

net entry 58, 65-67, 114

Neter 153, 155-157

new firms 8, 11, 15, 16, 38, 44, 49, 51-53, 55-57, 62, 64, 81, 82, 83, 85, 89, 90, 92, 94, 101, 113, 162

new industry organization 39

new markets 30, 39, 40, 76

new methods of production 39, 76

new products 39, 67, 76, 77, 92

new sources of supply 13, 39, 76, 77, 89, 101

new venture creation 5, 8, 11, 38, 47, 48, 53, 71, 72, 80, 81, 101, 150, 151 new venture formation 8-11, 15, 16, 21, 38, 43, 52, 57, 72, 77, 79, 80, 82-84, 89-93, 95, 96, 102-105, 107, 108, 114, 125, 128, 146, 148, 149, 150-152, 164, 165, 168, 170, 171

new venture performance 33, 174

new-firm entry 54, 83

niche 19, 39, 76, 90, 91, 102-106, 113, 115-117, 123, 126, 129, 147, 148, 159, 164-166, 169, 173

niche dynamism 90, 102-106, 113, 115, 116, 123, 126, 129, 147, 148, 159, 165, 166, 169, 173

niche shape 90

niche size 90, 91

Nightingale 12, 13

Norusis 151-155, 157

opportunities 6-11, 14, 19, 21-28, 30-38, 43, 44, 47, 49, 50, 68, 70, 72-75, 77-88, 90-94, 98, 101, 102, 163, 164-166, 169-171, 174, 175

opportunity 6, 10, 11, 14-16, 18, 22, 23, 26, 28, 35, 36, 39, 61, 67, 71, 73-75, 77-80, 82, 83, 86, 89, 91, 92, 107, 165, 166

organization inertia 46

organization theory 8, 9, 40, 43, 44, 71

organizational age 96, 97, 170

organizational change 45, 100

organizational environment 35, 38, 40, 41, 48, 83

organizational foundings 48, 49, 51, 53

organizational research 12, 42

organizational size 98, 99, 170

organizational structure 40

Orr 58, 62-67, 69, 90, 95, 104, 118, 119, 166, 167

Pennings 6, 173

Penrose 11, 14, 16, 21, 31, 32, 35, 37, 40, 43, 47, 71, 76, 80, 82, 83, 85

perfect information 20, 21, 29, 74

Pfeffer 40, 44

political/regulatory change 13, 76, 77, 173

population ecologists 4, 7, 8, 15, 44, 46, 49, 70

population ecology 44, 46-52

Porter 19, 33-35, 54, 55, 68, 90, 91, 165

potential entrant 53, 54, 61, 68

product differentiation 19, 20, 23, 54-56, 70, 93, 94, 169

profit opportunities 8, 21, 23, 25, 27, 36-38, 47, 73, 79, 84

profit opportunity 22, 23, 79

profitability 52, 60, 64, 65, 67, 68, 79, 166, 168, 176

proprietary knowledge 54

Pugh 99

Pull factors 7

R&D intensity 69, 93, 105, 106, 114, 119, 126, 130, 131, 147, 159, 164
rate of change 16
rate of entry 52, 57, 64
Rees 96, 99, 100
regulation 54, 90
research and development intensity 68, 93, 102-104, 108, 109, 113, 115, 118, 123, 130, 131, 149, 165, 166
residual 151-156
residual independence 153
residual normality 153
resource availability 23, 36, 39, 76
Reynolds 113
risk 27, 62, 146, 164, 166
Rizzo 7, 17, 21, 24, 25, 34-37, 71, 73, 74
Romanelli 14, 44, 45, 50, 51, 96, 97, 99
Rosen 16, 21, 29, 30, 34-36, 40, 43, 71, 73, 76, 87
Rumelt 12
sales growth 103-106, 108, 109, 113, 115, 116, 118, 123, 126, 129, 147, 148, 159, 164-166, 168
Sandberg 8, 33-35, 79, 85, 172, 174
Say 10, 30, 45, 50, 87
SBA 110, 111
scale economies 57, 58
Scherer 12, 13, 54-56, 59, 60, 73, 94, 118, 168, 173
Schmalensee 61
Schultz 21, 32, 35, 36, 71, 73, 85

Schumpeter 4, 7, 10, 16, 17, 21, 28, 29, 35, 37, 39, 76, 84, 85, 86-88
seizing opportunities 22, 171
Sexton 4, 10
Shapero 6
Shapiro 57, 58, 62-67, 69, 79, 104, 107, 120, 131, 167
Singh 7, 46, 51, 52, 96
Small Business Administration 110, 111, 123
small scale entry 58, 59
small-scale entrant 60, 63
small-scale entry 58, 59, 63, 95, 168
sources of change 38, 41
Spence 56, 60, 168
Star 127, 130
Starbuck 41
Stigler 14, 53
Stinchcombe 4, 6, 14, 45, 83, 96-98
strategic choice 43, 44, 46
strategic group 20, 68, 90, 165
strategic management 19, 20, 22, 33, 34, 44, 46, 174
strategy 14, 43, 49, 55, 68, 91, 97, 165
sunk cost 61
superior information 22, 25, 35, 37
superior knowledge 20
supply curve 13, 39
Supply determinants 6, 7, 15, 85, 172, 173, 175
Survey of Plant Capacity 110, 120
technological change 33, 35, 76, 92, 93

technological development
19, 76, 77, 89, 90, 92,
93
technological intensity
67-69, 92, 165
technological knowledge 22,
23, 36, 39, 76
technological progress 92
technology 13, 39, 92, 165
Terreberry 41, 43
Thompson 41
Timmons 3, 11, 93, 165
Triffin 20
Tucker 7, 51, 52, 96
Tushman 14, 44, 45, 50, 96,
97, 99
types of market change 75,
76
U.S. Department of
Commerce 13, 110,
120
U.S. Small Business
Administration 110
uncertain change 27, 28, 74,
75
uncertainty 10, 12, 24-27,
35-37, 41, 42, 50, 74,
75, 78, 86, 107, 166
union 100, 101, 105, 106,
109, 122, 126, 132,
143-145, 147
unionization 96, 99-106,
110, 111, 121-124, 126,
132, 147, 150, 151, 159,
164, 169, 170
USEEM 107, 111, 112, 121,
122, 173
USELM 107, 110-113, 115,
120, 121
VanderWerf 4
variable normality 151, 158

venture creation 5, 6, 8, 11,
38, 47, 48, 53, 71, 72,
80, 81, 101, 150, 151,
171, 175
venture formation 8-11, 15,
16, 21, 38, 43, 47, 52,
57, 72, 77, 79, 80,
82-84, 89-93, 95, 96,
102-105, 107, 108, 114,
125, 128, 146, 148-152,
164, 165, 168, 170, 171
venture formations 5, 8-11,
15, 41, 42, 44, 48,
51-53, 57, 62, 64,
70-72, 79, 82, 89-96,
98, 99, 101-105,
107-111, 114, 115, 120,
123, 125, 126, 127, 131,
132, 148, 149, 152, 159,
161, 162, 163-176
von Weizsacker 54
Weber 4, 6
Weick 46
Wenders 60
Wholey 42, 51
Williamson 55
Winn 166
Winter 47, 83, 96
Wortman 4, 5, 10
X-inefficiency 21, 25-27, 35,
45-47
X-inefficient 27, 34, 36-38
Yip 16, 33-35, 47, 58,
64-69, 76, 89, 92, 94,
168
Zammuto 19, 43, 46, 77, 90,
91